THE NEW
GLOBALIZATION

THE NEW GLOBALIZATION

RECLAIMING THE LOST GROUND
OF OUR CHRISTIAN SOCIAL TRADITION

Richard W. Gillett

THE
PILGRIM
PRESS
Cleveland

To
Madeline Janis-Aparicio
Maria Elena Durazo
The Rev. James M. Lawson Jr.

whose commitment to economic justice, great organizing skills,
and the conviction that "another world is possible"
have been deeply inspiring.

The Pilgrim Press
700 Prospect Avenue
Cleveland, Ohio 44115-1100
thepilgrimpress.com

© 2005 by The Pilgrim Press

Printed in the United States of America on acid-free paper

09 08 07 06 05   5 4 3 2 1

Library of Congress Cataloging-in-Publication Data

Gillett, Richard W.
    The new globalization: reclaiming the lost ground of our Christian social tradition / Richard W. Gillett.
        p.   cm.
    Includes bibliographical references (p.) and index.
    ISBN 0-8298-1682-8 (paperback. : alk. paper)
    1. Economics – Religious aspects – Christianity. 2. Globalization – Economic aspects. 3. Globalization – Religious aspects – Christianity. 4. Globalization – Social aspects. 5. International economic relations. I. Title.
BR115.E3G55 2005
261.8′5 – dc22

                                                        2005051524

Contents

Foreword

ABOUT TWENTY-FIVE YEARS AGO, Bernard Markwell, then a high school teacher in Chicago, told me that he was working on a Ph.D. on "the Anglican Left in the Episcopal Church in the USA."[1] I frivolously responded, "Will it be three pages long or four?" In fact, the work was a serious study of the influence of the Anglican social movement in Britain on Christian thought in the United States, with detailed studies of three major figures in the United States — Father Huntington, founder of the Order of the Holy Cross; W. D. Porter Bliss of the Church of the Carpenter in Boston; and Vida Scudder.

Some years later Bernard and I spoke at a conference on Anglican social thought from F. D. Maurice to the present day at a remote retreat center in Michigan, and we got lost in a wood. There were no signs, but they would not have helped as we had no idea where we were anyway, having been driven there from Ann Arbor. After some hours we bumped into Cyril and Marjorie Powles from Toronto, who were also lost. We eventually got back, but not before we had shared a vision of three streams of Anglican social thought — one deriving from F. D. Maurice via Stewart Headlam and Conrad Noel (my conference topic), one in the United States (Bernard's topic), and one from Hastings Smyth and the Canadian SCM (Cyril and Marjorie's topic) — all three fusing and disappearing from human eyes in the Michigan woods, and some doctoral student writing a thesis on us all.

My question, and our time in the woods of Michigan, draws attention to the fact that the long tradition of Anglican social thinking and action has not been so well known among Christians in the United States as in some other places. Many of those who call themselves Anglo-Catholics are fairly ignorant of it, focusing rather on the details of rite and ceremony, while mainstream Protestantism is often dominated by old-style theological liberalism. However, having spent a good deal of time in the United States since 1970, I realize that the Anglican social tradition is by no means extinct. There have been bishops such as Paul Moore and Kilmer Myers, pioneers such as Frederick Hastings Smyth, and, more recently, the work of the Episcopal Urban Caucus and the journal *The Witness*. My impression is that there is far more serious social theology taking place within the Episcopal Church than is the case in many other communities. Dick Gillett's book is an excellent example of this activity.

Since the 1960s, there has also been a growing movement of social theology within the Roman communion and within sections of evangelicalism. In the United States the work of such people as Dorothy Day, Thomas Merton, and Rosemary Ruether (in the Roman tradition) and of Jim Wallis, Ron Sider, and Walter Brueggemann (among evangelicals) has been important. Yet this tradition too remains unknown to most Christian people. In October 1996, the Roman Catholic bishops in England and Wales issued a pastoral document on the common good. The document, which some have claimed had helped to bring the Labour Party to power in Britain in 1997, was a very traditional one in line with the teaching of the encyclicals and pastoral letters on social and political questions that followed Pope Leo XIII's *Rerum Novarum* of 1891. Some of these have caused outrage in the United States. Paul VI's *Populorum Progressio* (1967) was denounced by the *Wall Street Journal* as "souped-up Marxism" because it described capitalism as a "woeful system" in which profit was the key motive of progress, competition was the supreme law of economics, and private ownership of the means of production was seen as having no limits and no obligations. Nobody familiar with the literature of Roman Catholic social doctrine would have been surprised at the general content of the 1996 document, which stood firmly within the mainstream of the social encyclical tradition.

What was surprising was the lack of awareness among many Roman Catholics that there was any body of social doctrine within the Catholic tradition. All the Roman Catholic laypeople interviewed by BBC Radio 4 in Coventry on the day of publication said that the church should not be involved in politics and that bishops should stay within their churches. The social tradition is, as the authors of a well-known manual call it, the church's "best-kept secret." I suspect that many of the evangelical Christians who helped to bring George W. Bush to power may also be unaware of the radical biblically rooted tradition within the evangelical world.

Dick Gillett's thinking is theologically rooted in the Anglican social tradition, and I want to reflect on this by remembering, and drawing attention to, the work and thought of my dear friend Dorothy Howell-Thomas, who so powerfully expressed it in her life and work. Her death in 2001 marked the end of a line of thinkers for whom certain lived historical moments were of critical significance.

She was one of the last significant Anglican social thinkers who united three different periods of history — the 1930s and the struggle against fascism and unemployment; the turbulence of the 1960s, when she played a key role in establishing the Church of England's Board for Social Responsibility; and her "retirement," the period from the 1970s to a few weeks before her death, the era in which we now live. The 1930s were formative years for Dorothy, having arrived in England as Hitler came to power in Germany. In September 1938 she became private secretary to the then-archbishop of York, William Temple. Her arrival at York coincided with Neville Chamberlain's attempt at appeasement, forever known as "Munich." Most people in Britain, and in the churches, including Temple and even Bishop Bell of Chichester at this point, supported the Chamberlain line. Dorothy was utterly opposed to appeasement. She remained Temple's secretary when he became archbishop of Canterbury in 1942, and typed his best-selling book *Christianity and Social Order* (1942), one of the few books in this field to have remained in print for many years. Temple began his first chapter with the question, "What right has the church to interfere?" Temple is a key influence on Gillett's theological perspective. Equally if not more important is the influence of the movement of industrial mission in Britain, pioneered by such people as Ted Wickham, to whom he refers. Why does this tradition, originating within English Christianity, matter and have relevance to today's world?

In an unpublished paper, written shortly before her death, Dorothy Howell-Thomas identified seven strands within the Anglican social tradition from its development in the mid-nineteenth century. First, the tradition of English ethical socialism, which can be traced to Cobbett, Robert Owen, and William Morris. Not a specifically Christian movement, it was deeply influenced by Christianity and by a sense of moral outrage against injustice. This stress on social ethics and moral outrage has been central to Anglican theology at its best and is evident in Gillett's book.

Second, the Anglican tradition of social criticism deriving from F. D. Maurice's Christian socialism. Maurice stressed the incarnation and the kingdom of God as central to faith and practice. His successors saw social critique as central to the church's spiritual task. Included in this tradition are such people as R. H. Tawney, though some have seen George Orwell as belonging here too. Among the bishops, Charles Gore and Temple were particularly important. Dorothy wrote:

> The stimulation to the church not to turn aside into a purely "spiritual" gospel in face of the massive problems of industrialisation and urbanisation of the 19th Century, but to be a "prophetic agent of change," continued as the need continued with the social problems such as unemployment of the 1920s and 1930s.

So the move from ethics and outrage to critique of policy and practice was at the heart of the Anglican social tradition. This too is evident in this book.

Third, the tradition of social analysis going back to Samuel Taylor Coleridge through Maurice, Thomas Arnold, and Edward Caird, master of Balliol College, Oxford. Both Gore and Temple were deeply influenced by Caird. Their profound belief in the incarnation, as interpreted in their period, informed their social conscience. But doctrine had to go hand in hand with careful analysis of social processes. This fusion of theology and analysis is also central to Anglican social thought, and Gillett develops it.

Fourth, Anglo-Catholicism and the "slum priests." Here, in the late nineteenth century and beyond, was a fusion of incarnational theology, sacramental worship with a strong emphasis on liturgical splendor, and a concern for the poor and downtrodden. In some places, one could see this movement as a prototype of liberation theology with a fierce passion for justice and a very local commitment. The Anglican social movement took its energy from the parishes, the smallest local units of Christian practice and consciousness. Gillett too is rooted in a bilingual low-income parish in Los Angeles.

Fifth, the organizations, the "little societies." These included the Guild of St. Matthew, the Christian Social Union, the Catholic Crusade, the League of the Kingdom of God, the Christendom Group, the Jubilee Group, and others. Anglican social thought and action has been nourished, guided, and stimulated by these supportive networks. Without similar "little societies," supportive networks of committed friends, I suspect that this book could not have been written.

Sixth, socialism itself (in those days people, including Christians, were not afraid to use the word) in the sense of a movement toward common ownership and control of the earth's resources. Anglican social thought, while not always explicitly socialist in a political sense, has always held strongly to the commitment to the just use of resources and has opposed exploitation and oppression. Again, Gillett stands within this tradition.

Seventh, and finally, Howell-Thomas laid particular stress on what is called "the Fifth Report." Published in 1918, this document from the Church of England was one of the major attacks on industrial capitalism. It makes much recent liberal social theology seem very mild. John Oliver called it "the outstanding expression of Christian social thought about post-war society"[2] while the American historian Bruce Wollenberg wrote that "it is difficult to overestimate the importance of the Fifth Report."[3] Dorothy commented:

> The Fifth Report was entitled *Christianity and Industrial Problems*. Published in 1918, entirely reprinted in 1927, its influence can be traced in the great seminal conferences such as COPEC

in 1924, and into a number of studies on Christianity and social order — in detail and in general — to say nothing of Temple's 1942 Penguin of that title. It is not stretching it too far, in my view, to see some of its influence on the principles of the Beveridge Report [which helped to create the British welfare state].

So Anglican social thought, in England at any rate, was concerned with the transformation of the social and economic order. All the preceding features were necessary to the publication of the Fifth Report, and to many others like it. Now we have another publication from within this tradition.

I have summarized this important but complex history in some detail in order to make a simple point: that for very many years, in Anglicanism as elsewhere in the Christian world, there has been a tradition of social critique and social prophecy that seeks to engage with, challenge, and confront the principalities and powers of the dominant political structures. It offers us practical guidelines for action in the future. It is to this task, nourished by this history, that Dick Gillett addresses himself in this book. This is the historical and theological background out of which Dick Gillett approaches the new global capitalism of the twenty-first century.

He makes it clear that, in the light of the shifts in global capitalism, the tradition now needs a rethinking. New situations call for new thinking and involve new duties. The best social theology, in my experience, has grown out of conflict over specific issues — slavery, racism, bad housing, AIDS, and so on. The current work arises in part from issues raised in Los Angeles around immigration, unjust working conditions, and the status of migrant workers within the new global capitalist economy.

Gillett is particularly concerned about globalization. Although the term is often used very loosely, what we are talking about is neoliberalism as a present manifestation of global capitalism. Of course, globalization as a transcendence of earlier national and local limits, in itself, is morally and politically neutral. But it does not exist "in itself": it exists as a particular mutant of postmodern capitalism, as an attempt to impose the interests of wealthy power structures in the West upon the world. As such it is politically imperialistic, environmentally unsustainable, and morally as questionable as were the earlier forms of capitalism out of which it grew. The late Pope John Paul II saw this clearly. Gillett raises issues that we ignore at our peril — and by "our" I mean the people of the entire globe. In my own experience of work over many years with migrant workers, I believe that what has been called "global social apartheid," and the "permanent structural violence against the world's majority" that is central to it, has led to the creation of a global, vulnerable, and when necessary, disposable labor force.[4] With Dick Gillett, I believe that this treatment of human beings as commodities is an obscenity that Christians, and all people committed to justice, should not tolerate, and should seek to end.

As in former years, the new situation calls for struggle, confrontation, and resistance; for detailed analysis; and for sound theology. My strong impression is that it calls too for a development of the Anglo-USA link,[5] not at the level of governments (though that will continue in its own questionable way), but at the level of those working at the sharp end of problems. We have much to learn from and to give to each other. It calls for a refocusing of Christian social thought and for the strengthening and deepening of the already existing vigorous and courageous Christian social action in both countries and way beyond them. It calls too for those in both countries who belong to the "confessing church" movement to work together against the terrible distortions of Christianity that, through their alliance with the culture of Mammon, continue to do such harm throughout the world. I hope Dick Gillett's book — which "urges the Christian churches to recover their social tradition" and to "reclaim lost ground" — will contribute to this necessary work.

Kenneth Leech

Preface

THE GENESIS OF THIS BOOK goes back to my seminary days at Harvard Divinity School and the Episcopal Theological School (now the Episcopal Divinity School) in Cambridge, Massachusetts, in the late 1950s and into 1960. Two books — one by an archbishop of Canterbury, the other by a pioneering urban priest in the British industrial city of Sheffield — then caught my attention and planted thoughts that have influenced my social and theological perspective ever since. The first was William Temple's small classic *Christianity and Social Order*, written in 1942. In it the archbishop succinctly and powerfully documented the continuation of Christianity's social tradition from the postbiblical period and on through the Middle Ages, showing that our tradition can speak effectively and authoritatively to the economic order of society. For me, that revelation was twofold. It meant, first, that Christians have not only the biblical tradition to call forth as the ground for the churches' commitment to social justice, but the entire two thousand years of our history if we will but explore it. Second, Temple's book served to highlight for me how grievous is our current abandonment of that comprehensive tradition, and the resulting embrace of a religious individualism that haunts the churches to the present day. The second book, *Church and People in an Industrial City*, by E. R. Wickham, written in 1957, was a portrayal of the substantial gap between the Church of England's parish ministries and the working people of the steel-making city of Sheffield. It documented Wickham's efforts to bridge that gap, and to begin through a new and innovative ministry (industrial mission) to understand the world of Sheffield's industrial workers, a world almost completely unknown or ignored by the churches.

In retrospect, I believe these two books set me on a path in my ministry to try to apply their lessons to the huge and complex arena of our contemporary economic order, and lately to the new globalization of the twenty-first century. Their messages ultimately stimulated me after my retirement from the parish ministry to delve into the history of the churches' social tradition which, as a seminary student, I had brushed over only lightly and with but little awareness.

At various times in my ordained ministry I've found myself able to exercise a ministry together with others that has demonstrated, even if modestly, that what we profess as socially conscious Christians can find significant engagement with the urgent challenges that the economic injustices of our present world present to us. I've included several of those moments in this book in the hope that they might shed some light on what is possible, and to encourage others.

In this book I make no pretense to being a church historian, nor any kind of economist. I confess only to being a reader of church history, especially when that history relates to social justice. As far as economics is concerned, I confess only to being an incorrigible news junkie and clippings cutter, along with attempting to keep up with significant writings on economics and globalization. I hope this will encourage people to feel that no elevated academic credentials are necessary as a prerequisite for the serious understanding of our social history as Christians, and for trying to understand the complex world in which we live.

All along the way in writing this book, I've received much help and advice from friends and colleagues who read individual chapters or advised on the book outline. Foremost among them are Brown Patterson, Frederick Borsch, Richard Parker, Kenneth Leech, Ian Douglas, Pamela Brubaker, and William Greider. Others who read chapters or supplied pertinent information and urged me on included Ann Blackshaw, Edmond Browning, Sr. Marie Clarke, Marty Coleman, Harvey Cox, Andrew Davey, Sr. Marie Dennis, Norman Faramelli, Brian Grieves, Madeline Janis-Aparicio, Emmett Jarrett, Alan Jones, Ross Kinsler, Michael Mata, Ted Mellor, Anna Olson, Scott Paradise,

Jere Skipper, Timothy Smith, Norvene and Doug Vest, and Kent Wong. My wife, Anne, has brought much more than a spouse's encouragement to this task; in reading several chapters she has not only occasionally corrected my spelling (spell check notwithstanding), but both in sentence structure and in clarity of expression brought to bear her excellent knowledge of good grammar. To her, and to all of the friends and colleagues mentioned above, I want to express profound thanks for their encouragement and confidence in the endeavor.

I'm also especially grateful to the Huntington Library in San Marino, California, who accepted me as a reader with access to their renowned collection, allowing me to pursue church history as well as some economic history that was relevant to my project.

Finally, my sincere thanks to the Pilgrim Press, and in particular to my editor, Ulrike Guthrie, who has been very accessible, a delight to work with, and a supporter all the way. And to Pilgrim Press's publisher and editor-in-chief, Timothy G. Staveteig, my special thanks and gratitude.

Introduction

EVEN BEFORE the catastrophic events of September 11, 2001, in New York City, Washington, D.C., and Pennsylvania had, like a massive undersea earthquake, triggered an existential tidal wave that immediately engulfed the world, a much longer and slower tsunami, one similarly transformative of the human condition, had been building across the globe. As with September 11, so this longer second wave — more than two decades in the making — likewise has profoundly affected the political, social, economic, religious, and cultural life of peoples and nations in ways that we have scarcely begun to appreciate.

This second tidal wave of change did not have its origins in a single event. It was not a new political doctrine originating in the halls of government. It was not orchestrated or directed by any plutocracy of industrial or financial magnates. Nor was it some new human or social vision of the people, born at the margins of political and social power. This wave of transformative change was too large and complex for any of those forces to manage or direct. Rather, it was the inevitable merging of the driving, inexorable logic of commerce and capital — a logic present in the Western world since Adam Smith — with new breakthroughs in technology, communications, and transportation. Beginning around the early eighties, this confluence began to shrink the globe even more dramatically than before.

This new global reality has not been eclipsed by the recent war against Iraq, the justification for which was that Iraq's presumed weapons of mass destruction presented an immediate and urgent threat to the United States. In the absence of finding any such weapons, it is now better understood that Iraq's huge oil deposits, coupled with its strategic position in the Middle East, were seen by

1

American policymakers as a chance to establish decisive American influence over that region. In this sense, of course, the war against Iraq was about globalization, albeit the globalization of American influence. But that is another story.

Before 9/11, it was the huge demonstrations in Seattle against the World Trade Organization meeting in December 1999, pulling tens of thousands of people into its streets from all over the world, that introduced the term "globalization" to the general public — though the reality of a "global economic order" goes back at least five hundred years to Columbus and the Age of Discovery. The term has come to describe both to its advocates and its critics this new global reach of the economic order that has appeared in the last twenty-five years. The protests that have continued since Seattle are forcing debate on the substance and direction of the new global capitalism. It is a debate that is intensifying over time. In New York, for example, in January 2002, the Davos World Economic Forum, consisting principally of elitist world economic, political, and academic figures, had to contend for the first time with sophisticated critics of globalization from within the conference as well as protesters on the streets outside. Since Seattle, and along with continuing protests in world cities, discussions and conferences have proliferated on the ramifications of globalization for world and domestic poverty, workplace conditions at home and abroad, environmental integrity, and the cultural and religious values of peoples. From college campuses and classrooms to trade unions to environmental groups and beyond, a multiplicity of nongovernmental organizations is also using the Internet to strategize, gather, and exchange information.

As governments and people struggled in the aftermath of the September 11 terrorist attacks to comprehend their implications, the connection began to be made between the rise of terrorism and this new phase which global capitalism has entered. Such a connection had been anticipated. It was strikingly captured on the cover of a book by Benjamin R. Barber in 1995. Titled *Jihad vs. McWorld*, the book's cover depicts only the dark eyes of an otherwise veiled woman holding a can of Pepsi. Barber wrote, "Jihad (loosely translated Holy War) is a rabid response to colonialism and imperialism and their economic children, capitalism and modernity." In other words, the underside of the new global economic order — its extensive disruption of local markets and employment patterns, the insinuation of Western cultural values that accompany the new commercial ventures, and the sudden infusion or withdrawal of foreign capital coupled with shifts of political power within an economically poor country — becomes the seedbed for deep resentments in many places across the globe. Such resentment, when coupled with a religious fanaticism unable to cope with the gray ambiguities of modern pluralism, finds tragic outlet in holy wars of terrorism against the nations of the West, most particularly the symbol par excellence of modern capitalism, the United States.

Confronted with such profound and complex changes of global magnitude, and with huge implications for political and military upheavals in the nuclear age, what is the response of religious leaders? More particularly, what is the response of Christian leaders and their churches? Aside from the occasional declarations of religious leaders at the highest level deploring economic exploitation and the violence of war as a response, and appealing for international respect and understanding, the churches at the parish level are largely silent. Issues of such vast complexity, particularly those relating to the economic order, are typically seen by the churches as being outside both their mission and their operating assumptions, these being that the Christian gospel is largely a matter of a person's faith relationship with God, and that the primary mission of the church is to promote such a relationship.

It is the contrary assertion of this book that the Christian churches in fact do have a religious base from which to address the great questions that center on the new globalization, that we in fact do have a strong and especially relevant social tradition. That tradition, embedded deep in our own history, draws its fundamental strength from the Bible itself. It is a tradition waiting to be recovered and used to address the principalities and powers of the global capitalism of the twenty-first century. But this great treasure has been almost completely obscured by the preeminence in the churches to the present time of a religious individualism that has its unintended roots in the Protestant Reformation — an individualism whose emergence overlapped with the emergence of capitalism as a new economic theory in the eighteenth century. These historical developments have worked together largely to obscure a central premise of Christian faith and action prominent in the church for seventeen centuries: that the Christian gospel was meant to apply to the totality of life, society, and the human condition, including the economic order itself.

This book urges the Christian churches to recover their social tradition, and to use it to address the global capitalism of the twenty-first century. In order to do this, we in the churches have some major homework to do with our own history. Where in that history is the witness strongest against economic and social oppression? And what moral and religious arguments were put forth to sustain that witness? How can we approach our tradition in ways that both reveal its cutting edges for justice, and also are applicable to the complexities of globalization? To help link our tradition with the new globalization I will explore the evolution in our history of three themes that I believe have particular relevance for a Christian global perspective: work, poverty, and *oikonomia*.[1]

A major challenge here is to begin to understand some of the principal hallmarks and components of this new global capitalism, and how they evolved. Over the last several years a voluminous literature on globalization has begun to appear; it will help us begin to ask what larger public policy options might be advocated to help move the globalization debate toward strengthening the most marginalized and vulnerable of our sisters and brothers. Just as important — perhaps more so — we will explore some leverage points the religious community might find at the local level, where some of the signs and symptoms of the new global economic order can be seen. These are all very complex questions, but they are not beyond our ability to address.

For happily the record shows that the Christian community has not been without witness in the decades leading up to the new millennium. There have been promising engagements with the forces of oppression and injustice from which we can take heart and learn. Moreover, we will review some religious projects and programs already under way that show both sophistication and promise in addressing the new global order. I will also share some organizing insights gained in my own ministry of over thirty years as an activist for economic justice in Puerto Rico, England, and the United States that are relevant to the new challenge.

Finally, even though the engagement of the religious community with the new global economy is a work in progress, and will be for the foreseeable future, we have the challenge of translating what we are already learning into outlines for educational programs and strategies for our parishes, schools, and seminaries. And we have the challenge of developing a new theology of globalization, a theology that arises directly from engagement with those who are both the victims of the injustices of globalization and its front-line leaders and spokespersons for a new, just, and sustainable global order. It is from them that we have the most to learn.

Chapter One

The New Globalization

An Overview

About twelve years ago at the plant where I worked, we had approximately 3000 workers. . . . We had contracts with General Motors, Ford, and big automotive manufacturers. But in the early eighties things started to slow down some. A lot of the operations were transferred to a non-union plant in Alabama. But they didn't stay in Alabama very long. They left there and went to a place called Agua Prieta in Mexico.

— Luvernal Clark, worker in Knoxville, Tennessee[1]

I now fear that the untrammeled intensification of laissez-faire capitalism and the spread of market values into all areas of life is endangering our open and democratic society. The main enemy of the open society, I believe, is no longer the communist but the capitalist threat.

— George Soros, multimillionaire investor, *Atlantic Monthly*, February 1997

It is a great sin to be born into this world a garment worker.

— Quotation from a woman garment worker at the
Young An Hat Ltd. factory, Chittagong, Bangladesh, in 2001.[2]

THE INTRODUCTORY PAGES of this book describe some of the broad changes manifest in the evolution of the new global economy: changes economic, social, political, and cultural. But if you were a moderately secure middle-class citizen living in a city or suburb in America or a country in Western Europe (acknowledging that this would represent a distinct minority of the world's population, more so if you happened to be white), what shifts might you have noticed in the last couple of decades that might make you aware of the global changes? Here are some changes this resident of Pasadena, California, has noticed:

- Our bank, United California Bank, has recently sent us a letter. It has just been acquired by Bank of the West. But not to worry, our money is safe (and I'm not worried — at least I think I'm not!). Before it was United California Bank it was Sanwa Bank, and before that it was Lloyd's Bank, and before that it was First Western Bank, all in the space of twenty-five years. Our money has (thus far) stayed put, and the bank building stays put. It's just that the bank's signs keep changing.

- In our city we have a huge new upscale shopping mall, architecturally very pleasing and inviting. It replaces a previous mall on the same site, one that opened in the late 1970s to similar fanfare and acclaim. For the inauguration of the new mall our mayor came and ceremoniously witnessed the wrecking ball knocking down the last of the old mall as he touted the new one. It features many stylish shops and restaurants. Almost all of them are national brand-name stores that can afford the high rental rates.

- If I go down Fair Oaks Boulevard between 6:00 and 9:00 a.m. on any day including Sunday, I see small knots of men, perhaps up to thirty in all, waiting on the street corner near the freeway. They are day laborers, virtually all from Mexico, recently arrived in this country and *sin papeles* (without immigration papers). They are hoping to be picked up by any contractor needing cheap manual labor. They will be paid by the day (and occasionally not paid at all), probably minimum wage or less, and invariably off the books. These men, desperate for work, are only the most visible sign of an almost 50 percent increase in the Latino population of Pasadena in just the past decade.

- In the last ten to twenty years we are finding tomatoes, melons, and strawberries in the markets at inexpensive prices in the winter as well as the other seasons. Much of this produce comes from large farms in Mexico.

- As is true across our country, I see everywhere in my city the logos of Gap, Banana Republic, Calvin Klein, Tommy Hilfiger, Nike, and others adorning the sweatshirts, jeans, caps, and shoes not only of teenagers but of ordinary folk up to and including senior citizens — free advertising worn willingly by the wearers.

♦ Last but far from least, homelessness in my town — largely unknown in the 1960s and 1970s — has become an accepted fact of life, as it has everywhere in the United States. I avert my eyes from the women and men pushing grocery carts piled high with their life's possessions or their collections of cans, bottles, and other recyclables. I try not to think about the new phenomenon of entire families, mothers with small children, being buffeted from place to place to place in search of shelter, work, or food.

The specifics of such changes as I've mentioned here would vary from city to city, and a connection with the larger global picture might or might not be clear. But even a moderately curious observer might wonder why such formerly stable institutions as banks, television stations, and newspapers are nowadays on a turntable of ownership; why commercial shopping centers can be built with great fanfare, then knocked down and replaced only a couple of decades later; and most poignantly, how it is that large and vulnerable sectors of the population, including immigrants, are now adrift on our streets, hungry and clinging desperately to life.

So my random examples may reveal some hints of the recent changes in the global economy: the increased disposability of people and their increased vulnerability in the job market, the increased transfer of financial and commercial assets, and through all and in all, the increased commercialization of everyday life. We are, in short, witnessing the accelerating domination of an all-engulfing global capitalism whose sole ethic is the market: what has been called the "commodification" of all of life. This global reverence for the power of market forces has reached such heights as to attain attributes of divinity, as theologian Harvey Cox has asserted.[3]

Of course, the sweeping changes the new economy has wrought in recent years have not been totally adverse. It is undeniable that recent globalizing influences have increased prosperity in many areas of the globe, including countries in the developing world. Globalization and its accompanying scientific and technological discoveries have also meant dramatic progress in the fields of modern science and medicine. Advances in transportation and communication have fostered a much greater awareness of the cultural, geographic, and historical diversity with which human beings are blessed on planet Earth.

But it is both the breathtaking rate of globalization in the last two decades and the clear and multifaceted inequities and disruptions it has produced, not only between the rich nations and the poor nations but also within nations both poor and rich, that demands a searching examination of the workings of the new global machine, or as William Greider calls it, "modern capitalism driven by the imperatives of global industrial revolution."[4]

What are the chief manifestations of this new reality? At least four are discernible: (1) the progressive impoverishment and disempowerment of tens of millions of working people and their families, both globally and in the United States; (2) the increasing domination by corporate and financial global interests of economic development decisions both worldwide and local; (3) the widespread assumption that such globalization is logical, beneficial, and in any case inevitable; and (4) the systematic promotion of material consumption as a primary goal of life through the expansion of commercial ventures worldwide and their accompanying advertising propaganda. Underlying these developments is a breakdown of cultural and social norms that, however imperfectly, had stood the test of time in many parts of the world, and their replacement with a deep sense of uneasiness at being surrounded by rapid and bewildering change, the outcome of which is not discernible. Let us look briefly at each of these areas.

The Poor Are Getting Poorer

It has long been the credo of classic capitalism that "a rising tide lifts all boats," and that the effect of a strong economy will eventually trickle down and result in the increased prosperity of those at the low end. This has never been entirely true even in the best of economic times for the poorest in the developing countries as well the poor here at home. Tina Rosenberg, in a detailed analysis of globalization and its impact on poor nations, summarizes information widely available in recent reports on international development.[5]

She reports that excluding China, the growth rate of poor countries was 2 percent *lower* in the 1990s than in the 1970s. Latin American economies grew in the 1990s at an average annual rate of 2.9 percent, or about half the rate of the 1960s. By the end of the 1990s 11 million more Latin Americans lived in poverty than at the beginning of the decade. In a similar analysis titled "The Mirage of Progress: The Economic Failure of the Last Two Decades of the Twentieth Century," Mark Weisbrot points out that gross domestic product grew in sub-Saharan Africa by 34 percent in the 1960s and 1970s. But from 1980 to 2000 when the machine of globalization was leaping forward, GDP per capita income in sub-Saharan Africa *fell* by 15 percent.[6] Major social indicators of the world for these years also showed significantly reduced progress in areas such as life expectancy, infant and child mortality, literacy, and education.

The distinguished urban sociologist Saskia Sassen, pointing to the appearance of a new kind of "global city" in recent decades, says that alongside new global and regional hierarchies of cities is "a vast territory that has become increasingly peripheral, increasingly excluded from the major processes that fuel economic growth in the new global economy."[7] In other words, the tremendous economic expansion by major corporate and financial institutions into every corner of the globe in the last two decades has not trickled down, but instead has tended to marginalize huge segments of the global population, a finding now widely documented. It raises crucial questions: Is this expansion dependent upon the existence of a large marginalized sector of the world or of our own country for its profitability? Or is the expansion in some way causative of the increased impoverishment?

A similar dynamic has appeared in the United States: a growing divide in our own country between wealth and poverty, increasing job insecurity, a growing number of people (now up to 45 million) without health insurance, and other negative indicators even as our economy, before the recent recession, was experiencing its longest period of sustained growth since World War II. For example, the Census Bureau reported that the number of people living below the poverty line rose in 2003 by 1.3 million, as the U.S. economy lost more than 2 million jobs since the year 2000 — a magnitude of loss not seen since the Great Depression. Meanwhile, in the recent proclaimed economic recovery, company profits have soared. New jobs created have increased, but significantly, these jobs are reportedly paying about nine thousand dollars a year *less* than the jobs lost during the recession. Moreover, jobs continue to move overseas at a significant rate. There is thus a recovery for profits but not for workers.

How do these statistics compare with previous decades in the United States? According to United for a Fair Economy, a nonprofit research organization in Boston, in the years from 1979 to 1999 the top 20 percent of the population increased its real family income by 42 percent while the bottom 20 percent suffered a *decline* of 1 percent. But in previous decades (from 1947 to 1979) the spread of real family income was strikingly different: the top 20 percent increased its income by 99 percent while the bottom 20 percent had an even higher income gain — 116 percent.[8]

The effects of the new globalizing influences upon the livelihoods of ordinary working people both at home and abroad can be illustrated by many examples. Two that are particularly instructive revolve around chicken and corn — as it happens, a favorite summertime barbecue platter for Americans. The production, processing, and marketing of chickens has long been acknowledged as involving some of the most deplorable workplace conditions for workers in the United States. Paid minimum wage or just above, working in near-freezing temperatures under assembly-line goals frequently impossible to meet, workers are typically threatened with reprisals or outright dismissal if they complain, or worse, advocate a union. These conditions have recently drawn the attention of the media, religious groups, and unions. In December 2001, Arkansas-based Tyson Foods, the world's largest producer, processor, and marketer of poultry-based food products, was indicted by the U.S. Department of Justice and charged with thirty-six counts of smuggling illegal immigrants across the Mexican border to work in its chicken processing plants. The plants, mostly located in the South where union activity is the lowest in the nation, have increasingly employed Latino workers, primarily Mexican immigrants. Deteriorating conditions in Mexico in recent years have resulted in increasing emigration to this country, where workers are willing to labor under conditions no longer tolerated by local residents.

In Mexico, corn has been cultivated for thousands of years as a basic staple of the Mexican diet. It is grown by almost one-quarter of the population, mostly on small plots of land. But for the last several years corn prices on the world market have fallen sharply. Corn farmers, once protected from foreign imports of corn, have lost that protection. New international agreements reached through the North American Free Trade Agreement (NAFTA) eliminated price supports for Mexican farmers — subsidies that once protected their livelihoods as well as ensuring domestic production of a vital food staple. The effect of the NAFTA agreement has been to open the gates to cheap corn imports from the United States, thus imperiling the livelihood of many small farmers and changing the shape and character of many hitherto more self-sufficient small Mexican towns. One report, by the Global Resource Action Center for the Environment, states that NAFTA has displaced 1.75 million Mexican farmers from their land, forcing them to migrate to other cities or to the United States.

Thus many such farmers go out of business, move to larger Mexican cities, or emigrate illegally to the United States — perhaps to end up on a Pasadena street corner looking for work, or in a Tyson chicken-processing plant in Arkansas.

The Growing Power of Financial and Corporate Institutions

A second hallmark of the new globalization is the sharply expanded reach and power of transnational corporate and financial institutions. Does this development represent merely a quantitative change?

Or is this something more: a qualitative change in the international workings of the world economy? Urban sociologist Sassen writes:

> The new growth sectors of specialized services and finance contain capabilities for profit-making vastly superior to those of more traditional economic sectors. ... This sharp polarization in the profit-making capabilities of different sectors of the economy has always existed. But what we see happening today takes place on a higher order of magnitude, and it is engendering massive distortions in the operations of markets, from housing to labor.[9]

In lay language what does this mean? It means, among other things, that the trading or transfer of money — thinking for a moment of money as a commodity — has become a huge global phenomenon in recent years. Stocks, bonds, currencies, and various forms of what banks and stockbrokers call "financial paper" have accelerated their movements around the world at an increasing pace in the last decade or so. In an early recognition of the prominence of money and financial transaction in the economy, political analyst and author Kevin Phillips called this new activity "transaction-driven amorality," or the "financialization" of the economy. "In the world of computer programs and tailored derivative instruments," writes Phillips, "where the money goes or what it does in its brief minutes, hours or days of electronic existence is morally meaningless: what counts — *all that counts* — is that it returns to its home screen a slightly more swollen slug of green or gray digits than it began."[10]

According to an International Monetary Fund report in 1993 the entire global volume of publicly traded financial assets (about 24 trillion dollars) turned over every twenty-four days — a rate that can only have grown in subsequent years. Yet this staggering volume of financial trading across borders was mostly transacted by just the world's largest thirty to fifty banks and a handful of major brokerages — a striking illustration of the increasing concentration of financial power and assets. Such a concentration of economic power both enriches further these already extremely wealthy banking institutions, and excludes de facto the participation of smaller national or regional banks. At least in theory, these could provide a business perspective more sensitive to national or regional needs, and also a more localized economic impact.

Related to these new global efforts both to move huge amounts of capital and to minimize national regulations or controls impeding that movement is the appearance, beginning in the 1970s, of offshore financial centers. Business and financial centers in such places as the Cayman Islands began to be created by the private sector in response to government regulation. They function principally as tax shelters, where financial transactions across borders can avoid the scrutiny of governments. We might envision such transactions as occurring in the balmy atmosphere of swaying palm trees and tropical breezes, but this would be an illusion. Although 593 banks were listed for the Islands in 1997, including 47 of the world's top 50 banks, there are not 593 bank buildings in these islands. Only 69 banks actually have offices there, and only six are "real" banks for cashing and depositing money.[11] Offshore banking centers, it turns out, are largely paper operations. Their existence underlines the extent to which the basic tax dodge has become accepted global business practice. It also shows how the decision making on such voluminous electronic business transactions, having found legitimacy in, for example, the laws of this British Crown colony of a mere hundred square miles, occurs in the faraway bank offices of New York, London, Frankfurt, or Tokyo; the people involved rarely, if ever, need to visit their tropical "headquarters." It is a discomfiting thought, this "dislocation of place" — now a common hallmark of the new globalization.

Prevailing Assumption:
The New Global Capitalism Is Inevitable

A third aspect of what we call globalization is the current widespread acceptance of the new global capitalism as logical, beneficial, and in any case inevitable. Not surprisingly, globalization's advocates are primarily corporate and financial elites in both the developed and developing world, leading international financial institutions such as the

International Monetary Fund and the World Bank, and governments in the developed world as well as some Third World governments. Also not surprisingly, the core Western notions of economic progress and technological innovation strongly permeate this favorable view.

The hallmarks of this type of globalization include a strong preference for free trade, the demand for broad governmental deregulation so that corporate decision making and the flow of capital may be less inhibited, balanced budgets as the norm for governments, and the assumption that technological innovation and the latest models of global communication networks are the sine qua non for a country's economy. In the United States, probably the most influential and unapologetic promoter of globalization is Thomas L. Friedman, foreign affairs columnist for the *New York Times* and author of the best-selling book *The Lexus and the Olive Tree*.[12] Friedman asserts that this new age is upon us with such compelling power and logic that we have little choice but to accept it. He declares that the historic debate between capitalism and socialism or its variants is over, and that the winner is free-market capitalism: "It is the *ideological* [emphasis mine] alternative," since only free-market capitalism is capable of generating rising standards of living in the world.

Friedman uses a metaphor that dramatizes this new reality: the Golden Straitjacket. Every country, no matter how rich or poor, or how disparate the gap between its wealthy and its poor, or how abundant or meager its natural resources, or how healthy or precarious its natural environment, must put on the Golden Straitjacket or be left behind. Putting it on means government deregulation, i.e., a maximum openness to capital from whatever source; fewer social services and less government in general; and workers' wages and working conditions as dictated by market forces (in practice this means the diminution of trade union power). In return for implementing these stringent measures, a country is rewarded by the streamlining of its institutions, the significant upgrading of its economic performance, and increased prosperity as a whole. And, adds Friedman, "as countries increasingly have to run balanced budgets to fit into the Golden Straitjacket, their economies become ever more dependent upon the

Electronic Herd for growth capital." The Electronic Herd is "all the faceless stock, bond and currency traders sitting behind computer screens all over the globe." In other words, countries have to submit to the decisions of these electronic technocrats, who in turn are guided by indicated outcomes of the computer modeling of international business and financial transactions.[13]

The engaging cleverness of Friedman's metaphors and his articulate prose can mask his sharply deterministic view of history's direction, specifically his conclusion that the struggle over political ideology is at an end. Particularly distasteful is his Golden Straitjacket metaphor which conveys a certain brutality — a cynical assumption that men and women are ultimately not free to chart their own political and economic destiny. But the popularity of his book, and its wide appeal to what many privileged and even not so privileged groups in both developed and developing countries would like to believe, is undeniable and serves as a sobering reminder of the challenges before us.

Globalization and Cultural Values

The fourth characteristic of the new era of globalism is its insinuation of Western cultural values into worldwide commercial ventures: a global convergence whereby consumers worldwide are pushed to adopt North American and European mass consumption habits of fast foods; fashion and footwear; toys (themselves mirroring Western mass culture); the latest entertainment trends in music, movies, and electronic games; and other commodities. Implicit in this new cultural homogenization is a crude but powerful Western value system: happiness lies in consumption (of every kind); efficiency and convenience become paramount (grab a McDonald's hamburger now if you're hungry — more efficient than preparing something at home later); and more important, aligning yourself with something new and trendy. Smoking Marlboros, or wearing Nike shoes or a Gap sweatshirt, immediately unites you with something bigger and alleviates a presumed sense of loneliness or alienation. All this is continually reinforced by watching television, where the power and seduction of global advertising gains sophistication and penetration year by year.

Such promotion strategies did not evolve by happenstance. Beginning in the 1980s a documentable change occurred in the thinking of key major corporations. They reasoned that because of adverse market conditions then becoming apparent, a successful business strategy would need to shift away from traditional production and sale of goods, and toward the marketing of brands themselves. Naomi Klein observes that in a strategy and marketing shift these companies began to market their *brands*, as opposed to the manufacturing of goods — a major switch to an aggressive advertising strategy. " 'Brands, not products!' became the rallying cry for a marketing renaissance led by a new breed of companies that saw themselves as 'meaning brokers' [*sic*] instead of product producers," writes Klein.[14] Incredibly, this insidious strategy is becoming aimed at very young children engaged in sports competition. A *New York Times Magazine* article titled "Why, Isn't He Just the Cutest Brand-Image Enhancer You've Ever Seen?" reports that equipment and clothing companies are giving children as young as four years old discounts for wearing their products. Reebok has introduced a commercial built around a three-year-old basketball player, a "brand-enhancer" that would make customers feel warm and fuzzy about Reebok.[15]

The ideological aspect of this development should be evident. A new "commercial civilization" is taking deep root: the "McDonaldization" of the world. Benjamin Barber describes it as a development in which the malls, public squares, and new urban "entertainment centers" of cities could be called the new churches.[16] They are complete with symbols and even a liturgy of sorts: logos, songs, jingles, and even soft evangelical exhortations to "spread the good news" of a consumer nirvana. It is an individualism — an American cultural characteristic identified back in the 1830s by that astute French observer of American culture Alexis de Tocqueville — gone rampant as it plays out globally under the imperatives of the new global capitalism.

So was Francis Fukuyama right when in his widely read book *The End of History*, published in 1992, he proclaimed the triumph of capitalism, which he saw as self-evident and as the sole political ideology of the future after the collapse of communism? The evidence of the new globalizing influences and their effects can appear all but overwhelming. But Fukuyama's view ignores two clear realities: the now incontrovertible awakening of voices and movements of dissent, and the lessons of our own past American and religious history at a time of similar upheaval.

In April 1999 at a national conference titled *Work, Economics, and Theology*, sponsored by the Episcopal Diocese of Los Angeles, Harvard University economist Richard Parker called participants' attention to the striking historical parallel of our own times with a similar disparity in America between wealth and poverty existing almost exactly one hundred years ago. The latter decades of the nineteenth century had witnessed the rise of industrial capitalism and the sharply increased concentrations of wealth and power as misery and exploitation deepened for the lower classes: a six-day workweek, twelve hours a day, with no unemployment or health insurance, drastic wage reductions in times of recession, deplorable working conditions, and an aggressive repression of workers' right to organize.

As with today, the government was strongly favoring the wealthy amid increasing and widespread poverty and unemployment. But as conditions began to worsen, the voices appealing for social reform began to be heard in calls for the breakup of monopolies, for labor reform, for women's suffrage, and for other social reforms. Not least among those voices calling for justice and a more equitable society were those of religious leaders. By the early twentieth century their efforts were being given theological recognition by prominent theologians such as Walter Rauschenbusch, and by pioneering activists such as Frances E. Willard, founder of the Woman's Christian Temperance Union,[17] and Episcopalian Vida Scudder, a professor of English at Wellesley College and a labor activist and organizer. The movement, which came to be called the social gospel movement, was much more than intellectual. Its insights came to permeate the theological positions of major denominations as well as the actions of clergy and congregations at the community level.

So as we face today the challenges of globalization we are not without historical precedent, at least in our country, and by extension globally. One hundred years ago the situation for ordinary working people in the United States seemed dire, yet as the new century dawned the conscience and voice of the churches and others began to stir and then to amass power and influence, until eventually the demands for social change reached Washington, and a new president, Theodore Roosevelt, launched reforms, in what later became known in American history as the Progressive Era.

Richard Parker's historical comparison has since been made many times by many observers. The lesson for us is that to know our history — especially our own history as people of faith — is empowering. We are not without precedent. After all, as Christians anchored in the tradition of the Old Testament prophets we believe in a God of history — a God who is yet *in* history.

Canadian journalist Naomi Klein was asked in an interview if all those young protesters at a huge Quebec City protest in 2001 against the World Trade Organization's meeting were not simply tilting at windmills. She replied that she saw them as questioning not just trade policies but the fundamental principles of capitalism as they were now emerging on the world scene. They reject passivity and fatalism, she said: "I call it the End of the End of History."[18]

In other words, history itself refuses to accept a death sentence.

This book is thus about globalization: what it is, where it seems to be headed, what it means for the social and economic well-being of the people of planet Earth, and how the Christian community is already responding. And it is also about history, more specifically our own Christian history, two thousand years of it, and the surprising wealth of relevance and power it carries for our current struggles. To reclaim this lost ground of Christian social tradition is of primary importance to the success of prophetic engagement.

The next chapter offers a brief taste of that historical wellspring before proceeding with the heart of this book: a more detailed analysis of some principal aspects of globalization together with some light that Christian tradition might shed on those aspects.

For Reflection and Discussion

1. What indications can you find in your hometown that might be signs of the new globalization?

2. What have you read in the newspapers in the past week or so that relates to the forces of globalization, and what did you make of it?

3. How might the issues posed by the new global capitalism (globalization) best be raised by a sermon in your church? What pointers could you give to the preacher?

Chapter Two

Christian Social Commitment

Some Historical Glimpses

Few people read much history. In an age when it is tacitly assumed that the Church is concerned with another world than this; and in this with nothing but individual conduct as bearing on prospects in that other world, hardly anyone reads the history of the Church in its exercise of political influence.

— William Temple[1]

Under the tense activity of modern social and industrial conditions the church, if it is to give real leadership, must grapple zealously, fearlessly and coolheadedly with the problems of social and industrial justice. Unless it is the poor man's church it is not a Christian church at all in any real sense.

— Theodore Roosevelt[2]

THE READER could be forgiven for supposing that the second quotation above comes from a clerical activist of our time calling for radical social commitment to transform social inequities, or a Latin American proponent of liberation theology espousing a preferential option for the poor. In fact its origin was in the second decade of the last century and the voice that of President Theodore Roosevelt, the trust-buster, social reformer, and churchgoer. His term as president (1901–9) came in the midst of the social gospel movement in the Protestant churches — a movement that fueled and undergirded the nation's commitment to social reform. Its seeds were sown by the gradually dawning realization amongst the churches in the closing decades of the nineteenth century that social inequities in the nation were becoming intolerable. Eventually they could not ignore the increasingly miserable plight of urban and immigrant workers in the nation's large cities, and the violent and deadly repression they were experiencing at the hands of industrial corporations grown ever larger and wealthier.

The social gospel movement found its most prominent theological proponent in Walter Rauschenbusch, but it reached far beyond his wide intellectual influence to extensive grassroots involvement by the churches. The *Columbia Encyclopedia* (1992 edition) states that the rigid dogmas of religious and economic individualism, although remaining strong, were everywhere put on the defensive by the movement. One of the most prominent voices of that time was that of Washington Gladden, a Congregationalist minister in Columbus, Ohio, who found himself deeply involved in a major coal strike in 1884. The experience transformed his perspective, and in 1886 he wrote, "The Christian moralist is...bound to admonish the Christian employer that the wage-system, when it rests on competition as its sole basis, is anti-social and anti-Christian."[3] In New York, James O. S. Huntington, a slum priest in the 1880s (later the founder of the Episcopal monastic Order of the Holy Cross), directly involved himself as an activist for workers and their right to join a union. Another Episcopal clergyman, William D. P. Bliss of Boston, in 1886 joined the Knights of Labor (a national labor organization that exerted wide influence in the 1870s and later). Bliss was also a member of the Church Association for the Advancement of Labor, of which Huntington was president. At its height the Church Association boasted forty Episcopal bishops as members. A major institutional and ecumenical step forward in social and political issues came when the Federal Council of the Churches of Christ in America was established in 1908. The Council adopted what was later called "The Social Creed of the Churches." It advocated the abolition of child labor, better working conditions for women, one day off during the week for workers, and the right to a living wage for every worker.

The injustices of late-nineteenth-century capitalism were not of course limited to North America. In Europe two landmark papal encyclicals, *Rerum Novarum* in 1891 and *Quadragesimo Anno* in 1931, inveighed strongly against laissez-faire capitalism and against an elite ruling class which controlled money, prices, and rates of interest that prevented national governments from protecting the well-being of their people.

I began this chapter with the late nineteenth century in order to draw attention to some striking similarities between the oppressive economic and social conditions of ordinary working people then and those we are seeing now, as well as the historic involvement of the religious community that then emerged in response — a response likewise beginning to be duplicated by the religious community in our era of a new global capitalism. Later chapters return to this important comparison.

The Early Church

The roots of the Christian social vision that stretches through our whole history are located in the accounts in the book of Acts of the first communities of Christians, as well as in various passages of the epistles, notably the Epistle of James. The Pentecost experience at Jerusalem, in which people "of every tongue and nation" experienced the outpouring of the Holy Spirit, found immediate application in the believers' sharing of their possessions in common (Acts 2:42ff) — an indication that the powerful spiritual unity they had experienced was also expressed at a material level. But as the primitive church grew to include the wealthy it inevitably began to experience a divergence of approaches to poverty and to the holding of property.

By the fourth century two divergent approaches to the radical demands of the gospel had emerged: the monastic renunciation of worldly possessions, and on the other hand the development of the practice of charity in the church, organized and unorganized. In Asia Minor, patriarch of Eastern monks Basil the Great (c. 330–79) embodied the first approach. Nonetheless, he established what would be called now a huge multiservice complex around his church and monastery. In one sermon he had a message for the wealthy:

> The bread in your hoard belongs to the hungry,
> the cloak in your wardrobe belongs to the naked
> ...the money in your vaults belongs to the destitute.[4]

So along with monastic devotion to God and service to the community (charity), Basil's vision was one of justice. Likewise Ambrose, bishop of Milan (340–97), consciously linked the mission of the church and its clergy with the active practice of charity toward people in difficulties — a position that would at first sound not unlike the position many churches today would espouse. But he, too, clearly voiced a perspective that echoed the spirit of Acts 2, one consonant with the ecclesiastical leaders of his time, both in the Eastern and Western churches, but one which today might be seen by many in our churches as an implicit if not explicit attack on capitalism:

> God has ordered all things to be produced so that there should be food in common for all, and that the earth should be for the common possession of all. Nature, therefore, has produced a common right for all, but greed has made it a right for the few.[5]

These are only two witnesses from an extraordinary cluster of ecclesiastical leaders in the fourth century from both East and West who drew consistently from scriptural texts on poverty and property. They set the tone for the social vision of the church for their own time. More significantly, these positions of the early church theologians are constantly cited later on by the most prominent theologians and canon lawyers of the medieval church in their own formulations of social and economic doctrine. Despite the accommodations inevitably made with the wealthy and powerful after Christianity became the official religion of the Roman Empire in the fourth century, their early positions constitute the beginnings of a comprehensive and holistic view of the mission of the church toward society.

The Medieval Period

With the emergence of the Middle Ages following the downfall of the western Roman Empire, a Christian vision of the social order came into clear and comprehensive focus. This evolution was part and parcel of a remarkable theological, intellectual, and political unity which emerged as the Catholic Church became the dominant influence in

Europe. It was admittedly an influence largely authoritarian, touching the lives of every inhabitant, Christian and non-Christian; the church used both its theology and its political power to build up its material resources, both in land and in the levying of fees of a wide variety of kinds. Yet its understanding of the Christian gospel was that the redemption of the whole social order — that is, the totality of society and the human condition — is the concern of the church, a perspective with which modern progressive theology, including for instance liberation theology, would agree. This perspective definitely included the political and the economic spheres of life.

It was Thomas Aquinas (1225–74), the great medieval theologian and "Doctor of the Church," who gave the fullest elaboration of this vision through his writings on the concept of justice in society. On property, for instance, he quoted Ambrose of the fourth century with approval: "Ambrose says, 'It is justice that renders to each one what is his, and claims not another's property; it disregards its own profit in order to preserve the common equity.'" The two medieval economic teachings most cited in Aquinas are the just price and usury. On the just price, he asks rhetorically, "Is it lawful to sell a thing for more than its worth?" He answers, "It is altogether sinful to have recourse to deceit in order to sell a thing for more than its 'just price,' for this is to deceive one's neighbor so as to injure him." In other words, price is not what the market will bear but what is just, i.e., reasonable in the recompense due the seller.[6]

The prohibition of usury, originally defined as the sin of taking money as a price for money lent, has historic roots all the way back to the Old Testament, and was repeatedly reaffirmed both in the early church and in subsequent church councils. But gradually in the Middle Ages the distinction came to be made between low interest and excessive interest, the latter being condemned as usury.[7] To our modern ears the idea of usury seems a quaint anachronism of history, so accustomed has society become in recent centuries to the lending of money at interest. Yet the practice of charging excessive interest was properly seen by the medievalists as involving excess profit and therefore as exploitation, and as such was widely condemned. Their perspective is well worth reflection — especially in light of the exorbitant amounts of interest that global financial institutions can command in the new global economy from borrowers of huge amounts of cash, developing nations prominent among them (and in light of the "usurious" rates charged credit card holders nowadays!).

Despite the strong and commendable treatises on justice and economic practice by Aquinas and other medieval theologians and by the compilers of medieval canon law, by the thirteenth century the Catholic Church had become institutionally grasping and ever more needful of revenues to maintain its expanding bureaucracy. It became less and less faithful to its own social vision. In response, new movements arose within the church to espouse religious poverty as a virtue, literally to model their Savior's life, and to address the neglect of the poor. Thus the ideals of voluntary poverty and solidarity with the poor first espoused by Francis of Assisi (d. 1226) spread widely throughout Europe in the thirteenth century, primarily through the establishment of the mendicant religious orders, most prominently the Franciscans and Dominicans, which established hundreds of communities throughout Europe. For a significant period these movements had the effect of both reminding the church of its primitive gospel roots and constituting a visible challenge to the increasing corruption and self-absorption of the Catholic Church as a whole.

The Reformation and After

As the merchant and banking classes of Europe expanded their dealings throughout and beyond Europe from the twelfth and thirteenth centuries onward, the medieval ideal of life with its unitary societal and moral views began to erode. Banking and credit became ways to safeguard money and expand profits. The church's positions on usury and the just price, although still given lip service well into the seventeenth century, were increasingly modified or ignored. By the sixteenth century, the century that saw the birth of the Protestant

Reformation, the new mercantile capitalism had begun to take firm hold in Europe.

The Reformation broke upon Europe following Martin Luther's Ninety-five Theses nailed to the church door at Wittenberg in 1517. A whole new understanding of what it meant to be faithful to God began to emerge: only through faith, rather than through the sacraments of the church dispensed by the priest, could the Christian obtain forgiveness and reconciliation with God. Luther himself never intended to cast off the institutional church wholesale; in many respects his religious views continued to be those of a medieval monk, which he had been prior to his conversion experience. But the exhilaration of Luther's new insight unleashed for many a sense of collective release from the corrupt and paternalistic authority of the church, and the liberating feeling that one could have direct access to God for reconciliation. It was a needed insight, one long neglected, and clearly the church was in drastic need of reform. But a steep price was to be paid in exchange: a dramatic diminution of the authority of the church in the new Protestant dispensation was now under way. With the salvation of the individual person emerging as a primary focus, the holistic societal vision put forth by the medieval church began to recede into the background. A new individualism — a belief that the person was autonomous — almost "prior to society" — came to the fore. Its roots were not entirely to be found in the new Protestant ethos; the more mainstream Protestant churches still maintained a social vision for the kingdom of God on earth. But in the evolving practice of Christian church members, the kingdom was now to be brought in primarily by the autonomous acts of individual members of the church, each acting according to his or her interpretation of Scripture and conscience. Thus by default the Christian churches as a whole began to cede responsibility for dealing with the larger social and economic problems of society to the secular authority, i.e., government, as well as ceding to it whatever social vision governments might consciously or unconsciously espouse. In Europe, with the publication of Adam Smith's *Enquiry into the Nature and Causes of the Wealth of Nations* in 1776, capitalism as a political theory came explicitly to the fore, influencing profoundly both public and private visions of human and social endeavor.

Notwithstanding the Protestant Reformation, the churches did not entirely abandon the more comprehensive view of their societal mission. The Roman Catholic Church has remained the strongest among the major Christian denominations in upholding the social redemption of all of society as part of the divine plan. And along with occasional commendable and comprehensive statements on the social mission of the churches, the Anglican, Lutheran, Presbyterian, Methodist, and most mainline Protestant denominations all have at various points developed significant actions for social and economic justice.

And now the signs of the times are pointing to yet another rebirth of this comprehensive vision of the gospel in this century of the new globalization.

For Reflection and Discussion

1. The "rigid dogmas of religious and economic individualism," says the *Columbia Encyclopedia* (quoted early in this chapter) "were everywhere put on the defensive" by the social gospel early in the last century. How is this "individualism" manifested in our churches today?

2. What is your opinion of the "just price" concept put forward by Thomas Aquinas? Could such a concept find practical application today? Why or why not?

3. What are the pros and cons of the emergence of "faith" as a principal cornerstone of Christian belief in the Reformation?

Chapter Three

The Evolution of Work

Man goes forth to his work
and to his labor until the evening.

—Psalm 104, Book of Common Prayer

[Work is] by its very nature about violence — to the spirit as well as to the
body. It is about ulcers as well as accidents, about shouting matches as well
as fistfights, about nervous breakdowns as well as kicking the dog around. It
is, above all (or beneath all), about daily humiliations. To survive the day is
triumph enough for the walking wounded among us.

—Studs Terkel[1]

AMERICANS WHO FOLLOW the latest gyrations of the economy in the mainstream news media have traditionally become accustomed to waiting upon the pronouncements of the chair of the Federal Reserve Board, a White House assessment by the Council of Economic Advisors, or a prominent economist to tell us what it is doing. Whether the economy appears to be strengthening or faltering, whether consumer spending is up or down, whether inflation is being kept under control, or whether unemployment is rising at the same time the stock market is rising (a paradox not often explained to us), most Americans are accustomed to defer to the experts. Thus described, "the economy" seems like some disembodied but all-pervasive entity that functions according to laws and trends comprehended only with great difficulty, if at all, by ordinary people. The high priests of these mysteries receive the reverence accorded them by the media when they make their oracular pronouncements; as the prophets of the Bible discovered, the high priests call down ridicule upon those who question them.

But the behavior of the economy — at *any* point in history, not just our own — is in fact rooted in certain assumptions made by persons and organizations holding the power to shape it. These assumptions have to do not only with how people behave in the economic choices they make, but how economic policies both public and private affect the larger well-being of the people as a whole. Political assumptions are made having to do with whether people have equal access to economic opportunity, whether and to what extent economic and social inequality must be addressed by public policies, and whether there are inherent human rights regarding poverty, housing, access to medical care, environmental protection, and other basic human needs. In 1996, the U.S. Conference of Catholic Bishops framed the issue of the economy in the United States in a moral context: "The economy exists for the person, not the other way around.... Economic choices and institutions must be judged by how they protect or undermine the life and dignity of the ... person, support the family and serve the common good," they said in issuing a ten-point "Framework for Economic Life."

Still, as laudable as these assertions of the bishops are, they are nonetheless made from within the capitalist ethos which the Western world has embraced for almost three hundred years. We need the daring and the imagination to go *outside* this ethos; we need to gain a wider historical perspective, one that allows the liberating thought that no single political or economic philosophy — whether it be capitalism, or communism, socialism, or another "ism" — has a lock on history for all time.

So it is essential to look carefully at history in order to understand how we have arrived at where we are today with regard to economic assumptions. It is likewise necessary from a Christian social perspective to examine our religious social tradition and its relation to the evolution of economic tradition over the centuries. To do this, we need not set down an economic history of the period covered, even in outline form; that would require a much larger book or books as well as an expertise I certainly can't claim. It is sufficient for our purposes to examine some key historical aspects of this economic evolution, from both an economic perspective and from that of Christian social tradition. To help us, I have chosen three themes through which to explore this relationship in this and subsequent chapters: work, poverty, and *oikonomia*,[2] "the well-being of the economic (global) household." As will be evident, these themes are not mutually exclusive but will overlap. This chapter reflects on work and its evolution.

What is work? How does it relate to the evolution of the economic order through history, specifically as it has evolved into the global capitalism of the twenty-first century?

The *Oxford Book of Work* defines it this way: "Work has an end beyond itself, being designed to produce or achieve something; it involves a degree of obligation or necessity, being a task that others set us or that we set ourselves; and it is arduous, involving effort and persistence beyond the point at which the task ceases to be wholly pleasurable."[3] The book then hedges this definition with a number of qualifications. One is that this is a relatively modern definition, one not descriptive of less complex societies in the more distant past, or in parts of the present developing world. Nor does this definition cover what we do in our nonremunerative work, whether that be tasks of the household, including that of raising a family, or other voluntary activity such as that in church or community. (As mentioned previously, the present book confines itself to the exploration of work as it relates to the evolution of the economic order.)

It seems undeniable that work is a central part of human experience in whatever age, from ancient times to the present. As Pope John Paul II's landmark encyclical *Laborem Exercens* (On Human Work, 1981) states, "[A person's] life is built up every day from work, from work it derives its specific dignity. . . . "[4] The roots of a Christian perspective on work go back to the book of Genesis, and continue prominently throughout the Bible and throughout Christian history. Given this prominence of work in our tradition, that so little emphasis is given in our churches to work as a moral and religious issue is indeed surprising.

Work in Primitive and Early Societies

For thousands of years prior to our era, work in human communities was that of hunter-gatherers or subsistence farmers and the associated tasks of food preparation, shelter construction, and the making of clothes and implements. Of necessity work was both collaborative and collective. The specifics of work life in primitive times and the division of labor between men and women are little known to anthropologists. But as such clans and tribes began to live a more settled life, the need for more skills increased — for example, those skills associated with building more sophisticated shelter, and the need for more efficient tools associated with a more settled agriculture.

With the rise of the ancient Greek and Roman civilizations, the complexity and sophistication of community life took a huge leap forward. With this leap came a new arrangement of work, and at least in Western civilization the documented rise of a new and well-organized phenomenon: slavery. Richard Donkin, in his book *Blood, Sweat, and Tears*, quotes Moses Finley in identifying three conditions necessary for the development of slavery.[5] They are worth stating not only to enable us to see the historical progression of work but also for their relevance to the American experience of slavery, and also to the work experience today in many places in the developing world. These conditions are that private ownership of land eventually evolves to require a permanent workforce, that commodity production and markets develop, and that there exists a scarcity of internal labor supply. By the time the slave had become an accepted feature of society in ancient Greek and Roman times, the ways and means of maintaining large numbers of people in slavery was well established. For hundreds of years in these classical civilizations slavery was the most common form of manual labor.

Work in the Middle Ages

Outside ancient Greece and Rome and until the Industrial Revolution, the vast majority of the population in Europe was scattered in rural and small-town communities. In the medieval village work was the primary activity that bound the community together. In a society that was to be predominantly rural until the early nineteenth century, such villages were frequently small, consisting of perhaps twenty to thirty families.[6] In both early and medieval times and well into the nineteenth century the workplace of most people was at or near the home. But by the time of the dissolution of Charlemagne's empire in the tenth century, the feudal system that was to characterize the Middle Ages in Europe had begun to emerge. It was a complex structure consisting of strict but not totally rigid class divisions, with nobility (and frequently clergy) at the top and the peasantry at the bottom. The work for peasants (serfs) could be that of working the land, or it could relate in various ways to the household needs of the lord of the manor to whom the peasant owed his fealty. And as it had been for centuries, it continued to be the case that workers and their families generally consumed or used the products of their own labor.

This latter relationship of peasant to lord is of interest to our examination of the evolution of work. Medieval historian Marc Bloch calls this relationship a basic arrangement throughout the social structure of feudal society. He calls it "the man of another man," meaning that the serf is the "man" of his noble lord. A serf would hold from his lord the land he worked and on which he lived, the produce from his plot providing his family's sustenance and also contributing to that of his lord. He might also (or instead) perform other works for the manorial estate. The forms that this arrangement could take varied widely, but its characteristic was the subordination of serf to lord, which was usually formalized in an elaborate ceremony of homage, in which the serf swore his fealty to the lord. Although subordination characterized this arrangement, it guaranteed land (the single most precious commodity in the Middle Ages), livelihood, and stability to the serf and his family, and thus a certain level of dignity to his position. Moreover he was not a slave, and could in fact buy his freedom or simply leave.[7]

So in a sense this medieval "man of another man," although frequently very poor, had more dignity and security than a twenty-first-century "man (or woman) of another" who works in a garment factory (whether or not literally held slave) in American Samoa, or an immigrant worker in a chicken processing plant in Arkansas. His poverty was not usually due to outright exploitation but rather to the primitive state of agricultural technology plus the vagaries of the weather, or to the economic disasters resulting from battles between warring lords.

With the increasing specialization of skills as the Middle Ages evolved, the medieval system of work, especially in the towns, developed into guilds for each work specialty. In the craft guilds such workers as weavers, carpenters, ironmongers, glassblowers, stonecutters, and other artisans developed guilds of their own specialty, setting standards for quality of workmanship, prices for their wares, rates of pay, and an apprentice system which guaranteed that the workmanship developed through years of work would be passed from one generation to another. The system engendered a strong sense of pride in one's work. Also the craft guilds protected their own members, functioning in some respects like a trade union, which centuries later modern trade unions would partly emulate. With the practice of designating a patron saint as the saint of particular occupations, the medieval church invested the guild craft worker with added dignity and a sense of being connected to the larger social and religious fabric. This furthered the long-established understanding of the dignity of work and the worker, which traced its roots to biblical authority.

Work in the Industrial Revolution

The birth of the Industrial Revolution is generally placed at mid-eighteenth century, when various historical trends came together, most particularly in England. Key technological inventions and improvements, the continued rise of the new "money economy" (capitalism), the new wealth and availability of precious metals (resulting from the explorations of European powers in the New World), and ongoing migration to towns and cities are among factors that historians mention. In Europe as a whole but preeminently in Britain, the hundred years following 1750 witnessed a quantum leap in the productive capacity of economies. In the process a radical transformation of work occurred, from an economy based on agriculture to one based on manufacturing and mass production. Not only the work people did, but also the goods they produced were transformed, along with the way work became organized.

Prominent writers in nineteenth-century England and Ireland were still passionately raising their voices against the social conditions caused by the transformation, Charles Dickens being the best known among them. Along with his better-known novels, his novel *Hard Times*, written in 1854, is the most explicit in its message. Here is his description of how a day's work begins in Coketown (said to be modeled after the Lancashire town of Preston):

> ...Pale morning showed the monstrous serpents of smoke trailing themselves over Coketown. A clattering of clogs upon the pavement, a rapid ringing of bells; and all the melancholy-mad elephants, polished and oiled up for the day's monotony, were at their heavy exercise again. Stephen bent over his loom, quiet, watchful and steady. A special contrast, as every man was, in the forest of looms where Stephen worked, to the crashing, smashing, tearing piece of machinery at which he labored.

Then Dickens, addressing the reader, gives us his subtle but passionate insight into the dangers to humanity of the new conditions:

> Never fear, good people of an anxious turn of mind...set anywhere side by side, the work of God and the work of man; and the former, even though it be a troop of Hands of very small account, will gain in dignity from the comparison.[8]

In other words, despite these conditions, the workers will maintain their humanity.

But two centuries before Dickens, in the period following the twilight of the Middle Ages and well before the first glimmer of a new age of manufacturing appeared, the work that human beings did began to be more sharply defined. In the sixteenth century for instance, the lines between work and leisure, employed and unemployed, and work and home were still indistinct. But gradually as scientific invention and the flow of money increased, it became possible to think of "work" in the abstract. Thus, in 1651 the English philosopher Thomas Hobbes could write, "A man's labor is a commodity exchangeable for benefit as well as any other thing."[9] It was becoming common to accept that productive work was the basis of civilization. Labor as a commodity is an idea so commonly accepted among us today that we find it hard to imagine it could ever have been otherwise. This new perspective was closely related to the emergence of a new entrepreneurial class and the rise of capitalism.

A cluster of new inventions occurring within about a fifty-year period in eighteenth-century England constituted a huge leap forward into the transformation of the productive process. In that period coal replaced wood as the primary fuel, the steam engine was invented, the fulling mill emerged, and the inventions of the flying shuttle, the spinning jenny, the water frame, and the power loom combined to facilitate the establishment of the textile mill towns in Lancashire and other areas. By 1780 there were 120 textile factories in England; the balance of productive power had shifted from the artisan weaver working at home to the merchant-owners of the textile factories, and England became almost overnight the greatest producer of textiles in the world.

In human terms the cost of the new factory system was enormous, and — we need to be reminded — was also borne by children, who were recruited from the poorhouse at ages as young as seven. Because of their small frames, they were used as chimney sweeps, sometimes under unspeakably brutal conditions and long hours, or harnessed like sled dogs to pull mine carts in the narrow coal or slate mine tunnels. But children were also employed in the cotton mills, frequently with other family members. To one contemporary observer they appeared "almost universally ill-looking, small, sickly, barefoot and ill-clad. Many appeared to be no older than seven. The men, generally from 16 to 24, and *none aged* [emphasis mine], were almost as pallid and thin as the children."[10]

Yet so strong a grip did the Puritan work ethic, combined with the new rationalization of the manufacturing process, exercise upon the society at the time that incredibly the factory system could even be lauded in religious terms. Andrew Ure, writing in 1835 on "The Moral Economy of the Factory System," states the urgent need of "training human beings to renounce their desultory habits of work and to identify themselves with the unvarying regularity of the complex automaton." These disciplinary virtues must be achieved by inculcating "the great lesson . . . that man must expect his chief happiness not in the present, but in a future state." Work must be therefore undertaken as a "pure act of virtue . . . inspired by the love of a transcendent being."[11]

Now enter Karl Marx (who could understandably conclude from such pronouncements as those of Andrew Ure that religion is the opiate of the people), who took the understanding of the human enterprise of work to an extreme, claiming it as the defining feature of the human race. Marx, likewise observing the emerging condition of industrial labor, wrote in 1844 that "Labour produces workers of wonder for the rich, but nakedness for the workers. It produces palaces, but only nakedness for the worker; it produces beauty but cripples the worker. . . . "[12] Observing this condition of the industrial working class of nineteenth-century Europe, Marx referred to it as "alienated labor." Labor is alienated, he said, because the worker, the direct producer of material goods, is not master of his or her means of production, nor of the conditions under which the work is performed, nor of the final result of these efforts. Marx's monumental writings, principally *Das Kapital*, launched a new economic theory, one grounded in a historical analysis of the development of work. Its central focus was the worker and the worker's labor in relation to the social and economic order, and it laid the groundwork for the confrontations of the two dominant economic theories of the twentieth century: socialism and capitalism.

Notwithstanding the emergence of this new economic theory, by the mid-nineteenth century the innovativeness of the new production processes which England had introduced had begun to be surpassed by the United States as it, too, began to industrialize. In the latter decades of the nineteenth century the rationalization of the manufacturing process developed further and was given a great leap forward by the theories and applications of Frederick Winslow Taylor of Philadelphia. Taylor, a man said to be imbued with the Protestant work ethic, worked to match the capability of machines — which were increasingly being standardized — with the standardization of human movements. The latter were dissected and categorized to a minute degree, the idea being that the human being in the workplace is to become as much like a machine as possible. Taylor's time-and-motion studies, in which the use of a stopwatch is central in order to time specific movements of a worker at his task, began to be widely applied in the first decade of the twentieth century.

With the introduction by Henry Ford of the automobile assembly line to mass produce the Model-T Ford in 1914, the line worker experienced "Taylorism" in its most advanced mode. By all accounts it was a fairly brutal work experience, the chief evidence being a very high turnover rate of assembly-line workers. Henry Ford saw early on that this turnover could not be sustained, and took a dramatic and unexpected step, that of raising the pay of his workers to five dollars a day for an eight-hour day, a very high wage at the time. But as Richard Donkin observes, "It was the equivalent of a Faustian bargain for the worker, sacrificing his individuality for the means to improve the material existence of his family and himself. . . . It was a different image of the promised land from that of the Pilgrim Fathers." Concludes Donkin: "Taylorism and Fordism transformed factory working so completely that the systems together must be viewed as perhaps the most enduring societal change of the twentieth century."[13]

We should be reminded, however, that these developments of the late nineteenth and early twentieth centuries did not go unchallenged.[14] Even before the social gospel movement blossomed into full flower in the early twentieth century, prominent clergy were questioning the worsening plight of workers. Bishop Henry Codman Potter of New York issued a pastoral letter in 1886 concerning the current labor troubles, a statement (albeit somewhat dense in the reading) said to be one of the most influential documents of early social Christianity:

> When capitalists and employers of labor have forever dismissed the fallacy, which may be true enough in the domain of political economy, but essentially false in the domain of religion, that labor and the laborer are alike a commodity, to be bought and sold, employed or dismissed, paid or underpaid, as the market shall decree ... then, but not till then may we hope to heal grave social divisions, concerning which there need to be among us all, as with Israel of old, "great searchings of heart."[15]

Work in the Last Fifty Years

In the decades immediately following World War II manufacturing jobs in heavy industry continued to be the mainstay of the American economy and were heavily unionized. Then about 1980, jobs in the service sector began to grow significantly as the manufacturing sector declined steeply both in the United States and in Europe. In contrast, manufacturing has grown markedly in developing countries since the Second World War.

In the United States in the last twenty years the service sector has seen a large increase in numbers of low-wage nonunion hotel workers, health-care workers (except nurses), security guards, janitors, food-service workers, retail clerks, and the like, together with higher-paid "information age" technicians throughout the economy. At about the same time we have seen the marked growth of "contingent" or temporary workers who are hired or laid off according to the rapidly changing needs of the economy. Such workers typically lack health benefits and are frequently low-wage and also nonunion. In Los Angeles, workers such as hotel and food-service workers, janitors, airport security screeners, and nursing-home assistants find their wage base eroding — working at or near minimum wage, lacking health benefits, and working in a clearly antiunion environment. Added to this is the recent tendency of employers nationally to order "job speedups" in order to increase productivity. Cited in a front-page article in the *Los Angeles Times*, Christina Román, a worker with twenty-four years of experience in packing airline meals, said she was fired because her bosses now wanted work done in three hours that used to take five. And an African American man in his early twenties working as an airport security screener, interviewed at a church near Los Angeles International Airport and making just above minimum wage, voiced his extreme frustration with job pressures, saying over and over, "There's just no respect."[16]

No respect. This refrain from low-wage workers across the job spectrum is constant but seldom acknowledged. As an intangible it is not given much weight, yet the call for respect and dignity for workers in the workforce is a cry issuing from the gut (as Studs Terkel's poignant words quoted at the head of this chapter testify). It is a cry not new among the working class, one at least as old as the Industrial Revolution.

In the developing world the last twenty years have seen the burgeoning of manufacturing plants as global corporations seek lower production costs overseas, principally in the form of cheap labor. Writing about extensive visits to factories in developing nations, William Greider speaks of encountering exploited young people, peasant children turned into low-wage industrial workers and struggling to understand their own condition.[17] He also reports on the enormous human cost of industrial accidents. For example, Thailand acknowledged that workplace injuries ballooned from 37,000 to over 150,000 in a five-year period ending in 1992. Even more shocking was a finding in March 2001 of the National Labor Committee, a nonprofit organization advocating workers' rights, that a Korean-owned factory in American Samoa had held 251 "guest workers" as virtual "slave laborers" for a period of two years. The Daewoosa factory sewed clothes under subcontract to J. C. Penney, Wal-Mart,

Sears, and Target stores. This widely publicized scandal, like the earlier American scandal in 1995 in which Thai workers were barricaded in a garment factory in El Monte, California, was a grim reminder that indentured servitude is not a relic of the history books. In the case of American Samoa, the federal court found the owner guilty of human trafficking and sent him to prison; it also ordered payment of back wages to the workers. But thus far, of the American companies involved in the subcontracting, only J. C. Penney has agreed to pay workers their back wages; the others have stalled.

So in the last twenty years the work experience of many workers both domestic and foreign is in striking contrast to that of the early postwar decades. In the 1950s and '60s traditional blue-collar industry, still the economic and industrial backbone of the American economy, was also considered the blueprint for the economic development of the poor nations. Work in automobile plants, steel plants, aerospace plants, mining, and subsidiary manufacturing plants was both well-paid and generally unionized. It was also the path out of poverty and into a stable middle class for large numbers of African Americans and Latinos with only a high school education. The work itself was usually relentless, monotonous, and brutal — a test of a worker's physical and mental endurance. Steelworker Mike Lefevre described his job to interviewer Studs Terkel: "It isn't that the average working guy is dumb. He's tired, that's all. . . . The first thing that happens at work: when the arms start moving the brain stops. . . . I'm a dying breed. A laborer. Strictly muscle work . . . pick it up, put it down, pick it up, put it down. We handle between forty and fifty thousand pounds of steel a day."[18]

Yet for such workers there was also a certain pride in just surviving. And that experience of enduring physical hardship, mental boredom, and occasional harassment by supervisors also engendered a strong camaraderie among the workers. A worker was also conscious that as a steelworker or auto worker, for example, he or she (women also worked the assembly lines) was a part of an industry considered central to the economic well-being of the country.

In 1966–67 as an apprentice clergyman in training in England for Industrial Mission, I had the privilege of regularly visiting a large steel factory in Manchester which made railroad wheels. The hard physical work, the monotony, the grit and grime and the noxious smell of the factory floor were all present there in Britain as they would be in my own country. On one occasion I chanced to have a conversation with a worker whose job for twenty years had been confined to driving a small vehicle back and forth between a bank of gas furnaces heating steel ingots to orange-white temperatures. His vehicle would regularly pluck one out of a furnace and deliver it to a huge steam hammer. With two or three tremendous blows, the hammer would transform the ingot into the beginnings of a railroad wheel. When I caught the worker on his tea break, I asked him what it was like doing that work. He replied that this particular day, after twenty years of doing this work, was his last day at work; he was retiring. "What are your thoughts on your last day of work?" I asked. His answer was instantaneous and quietly triumphant: "I've beat the system," he replied. He meant that he had survived; that he had endured a "system" which by all odds should crush a human being, but he had beaten the odds.

Thus, within reach of the memory over the last fifty years in the United States and the rest of the "First World" of the developed nations is a time of relative stability, when the smokestack industries (so named for all the pollution they generated) symbolized prosperity and the industriousness of workers (for all they endured); followed by a time beginning in the 1980s of dramatic change in the structure and composition of the workforce. With this change came a corresponding psychological as well as physical dislocation of workers as both their job insecurity and their poverty increased significantly, and as their sense of connectedness to some larger national purpose largely disappeared. In the poor nations this sequence is more complex, but it is accurate to say that from the worker's point of view earning a livelihood today is much more precarious and is more subject to economic conditions beyond the worker's control.

In her important book *Beyond the Bottom Line*, Paula Rayman asks a crucial question: can we achieve dignity at work in the modern economy? Acknowledging that the search for dignity at work has religious roots, she asserts that dignity means a recognition of each human being's intrinsic worth. She identifies three pillars of dignity in the workplace: self-respect, adequate remuneration, and the connection of one's work with some larger social purpose. She places these assertions alongside the grim realities of modern work life. Today, she says, the fundamental arithmetic of the family has changed. In today's two-career family there are three jobs, two paid and one unpaid (that of tending the household, including the raising of children), but still only two people to do them. Or grimmer still, in the case of many single-parent workers, two or even three jobs and one person to do them, *plus* raise a family.[19]

So the answer to Paula Rayman's question is by no means clear at this juncture in history. Nonetheless, the question is a crucial one for the well-being of all working families, and is one the religious community is especially challenged to address — not least from the perspective of its own tradition regarding work and human fulfillment.

For Reflection and Discussion

1. Given that work is a central part of the human experience, why do you think so little emphasis is given in our churches to work as a moral and religious issue?

2. Reflect on your own work experience present or past, and relate it (or not) to Pope John Paul II's statement that "a person's life is built up every day from work, from work it derives its specific dignity."

3. Do you think more or fewer people find satisfaction in their work than was the case fifty years ago? Why?

Chapter Four

Toward Religious Engagement

The World of Work

As a priest, because Christ has chosen me, I must bind this world to the invisible love of the Spirit, not in the delirious optimism of a humanity consecrated to the worship of labour, but by the gathering together in the same faith, of the Man-God, of men, of these labourers [i.e., his fellow factory workers] who change the shape of the world and are themselves changed in turn by their work.

—A French worker-priest speaking of his life in the factory in 1954[1]

The lesson is so painful and hard that industrial missioners themselves resisted it. And yet it is simple and obvious: that is, the value commitments of industrial culture are false and point the world toward disaster. If the Church is to serve the truth and offer health and hope, it must challenge these values and offer an alternative way of life.

—The Rev. Scott I. Paradise, Industrial Missioner from 1953 to 1992[2]

IT IS NOT WIDELY RECOGNIZED that there have been significant programmatic efforts by the churches since the end of World War II to understand and engage with the industrial workplace and the lives of the men and women working in its factories. In France for a period of ten years (1944–54) almost a hundred priests of the Catholic Church went into the factories of Paris as workers in a coordinated undertaking called "Mission de Paris" with the active blessing and support of the cardinal of Paris. This attempt by the church in France to understand and actually experience the industrial workplace of the mid-twentieth century was imitated in England as "Industrial Mission" but with a different emphasis, launched in 1944 by an Anglican priest with the strong support of his bishop. In 1956 in America the attempt to bridge the gap between the world of work and the world of religion found yet another incarnation in the founding of the Detroit

Industrial Mission by an Episcopal priest, in the automobile capital of the world. It too was supported by his bishop.

Other attempts by the churches to engage the world of work are less well known in the United States than these three, but nonetheless had real significance. From the 1950s to the 1970s, for example, urban-industrial missions were undertaken in large cities in Africa, Asia, and Latin America, where the economics and technology of Western industrialization were rapidly penetrating the emerging nations, especially the former colonial possessions of Europe. As early as 1958, the first ecumenical Asian Conference on Industrial Evangelism was convened in Manila. Although focused more broadly than just on the workplace, its discussions revealed awareness of the dangers inherent in unbridled economic change and the exploitation of working people that was already happening.

In this chapter we look mainly at the undertakings in France, Britain, and the United States that attempted to focus on the industrial workplace in this fifty-year period.

Wartime Paris (1944) found Catholic priests already working in factories as workers. Deeply conscious of the profound alienation of the French working class not only from the French bourgeoisie but from the church, they had entered fully into factory work as workers — not to preach or counsel but simply to "be a presence." Remarkably, the aims and ideals of these worker-priests were fully embraced by Cardinal Suhard, archbishop of Paris, who established the "Mission de Paris" in a pastoral letter promulgated in 1947. They are to live with workers and as workers, renouncing their priestly stipends, livings, and privileges, the cardinal said. He challenged them "to be a worker among workers, as Christ was a man among men, to link one's destiny with their destiny, one's life with their life, to be the one among them whose hopes go farther than their hopes."[3]

This they did. Although their efforts to strongly identify with the factory workers resulted in no discernible return to the church by the workers, the priests themselves were profoundly transformed by the experience. Some found a new spirituality. Many became involved in trade union activities, some attained office in communist unions.

Others participated in demonstrations, some of them being sacked from their jobs along with their fellow workers. Many continued to celebrate the Eucharist, but at a worker's kitchen table as opposed to the marble altar and trappings of a parish church.

Their experiment ended in 1954, when the Vatican shut it down. It said that in the clergy's full participation in the factory life of the worker, their priesthood was being compromised. There were also other fears, namely that the church would become "infected with the communist virus," and that the priests' activities presented a threat to the traditional structure of parish life. It is true that the Catholic hierarchy by and large were deeply aware that the church in France had lost the industrial masses wholesale and desired their return. But as E. R. Wickham (founder of the British Industrial Mission movement) pointed out, "They [the hierarchy] had genuinely desired an apostolate at the heart of the working class; they were appalled at the ducklings they had hatched."

Thus, it was generally acknowledged that the undertaking had failed in its mission to bridge the gap between the church and the working class in France. But the impact of the experiment brought to many Christians an awareness for the first time that such a world of work existed, and should in fact be a chief concern of the church.

It was E. R. (Ted) Wickham, deeply inspired by the French example, who was sent to Sheffield, the heart of industrial England, to establish an "Industrial Mission" in 1944 at the urging of his bishop, who was concerned about the gap between the world of industry and the church. By 1953 there were four full-time clergy at the Sheffield mission, with over a hundred discussion groups going on in the mills and offices of that historic steel town, the heart of British steel production at that time.[4] Over the next several years Industrial Mission projects were established in many of the major industrial areas of the country, attracting widespread interest both in and beyond the church. The earliest years of the new movement focused simply on reaching the working class and their managers on factory floors and in offices, with the goal of beginning to listen, observe, and enter into dialogue. As with the French experiment, the British effort recognized the gap between the working class and the church, both countries having minuscule representation (with the exception of the Methodist Church in Wales) of ordinary workers in their parishes. Ted Wickham warned me in Manchester, as I started my Industrial Mission apprenticeship in 1966 at the Taylor Steelworks in that city, not to expect quick results: "You'll be mistaken if you think you're going to get them to come to church!"

Throughout the 1960s and most of the '70s, Industrial Mission-ers in Britain developed discussion groups and conferences involving labor and management, focused on the issues of factory life and work, the goal being to humanize the industrial workplace. Accord-ing to Christopher Beales, a British former Industrial Missioner, the movement's vision, embraced passionately and with great hopes by the missioners, was that "Industrial Mission could influence — and Christianize — the workplace, and therefore the economy, and there-fore society...."[5] It appeared to them that a new missionary field had been discovered, and a new and innovative ministry launched to explore the world of industry and, if possible, convert it.

Interestingly, in an early essay on Industrial Mission, Wickham, by then an assisting bishop in Manchester, had voiced doubts not that the church could help provide a significant bridge between church and the industrial workplace — he strongly believed it could — but doubts that the institutional church, being overwhelmingly parish-centered, could exert significant influence on "the fluid forces of modern in-dustrial society" — thus acknowledging the existence of a huge gap between parish ministry and the deep problems of industrial society. Wickham and others worked diligently to create a national church strategy focused on the urban conglomerate to "influence the influ-encers of society." In any such strategy, he concluded, some new deployment of people-power, some new expression of ministry, will be required. He had hoped to build up in the church a team of special-ists, trained and nurtured in the context of a Christian social analysis of society, and highly conscious of the realities of the industrial work experience. In Wickham's scheme, Industrial Mission would be but one manifestation of such an effort. For Industrial Mission he envisioned the establishment in England of a nongeographical diocese composed of specific projects, overseen by a bishop. But such dreams did not come to fruition, and over time he found widespread indifference, incomprehension, or outright hostility among church leadership to his endeavors.

As the 1980s dawned, traditional heavy industry in Britain was in the throes of a broad collapse (as was heavy industry in the United States) along with a sharp political swing to the right under the new conservative prime minister, Margaret Thatcher. Massive unemployment ensued, and the collapse of heavy industry shattered much of the Industrial Mission work (and literally the workplace, in some cases), and also the consensus among the industrial missioners that the churches, working for the common good together with industry, labor, and government, could in fact help bring about a more human and just industrial order. No one had anticipated that this massive and seemingly permanent industrial "machine" would go down so quickly and with such devastating effect.

The postwar British attempt to bridge the gap between the church and the world of industrial work via "church presence in industry" thus largely collapsed. Today, reports Beales, Industrial Mission in Britain has "lost the plot": it is no longer there in a strategic sense. The factory work of the Industrial Missioners of the postwar decades largely disappeared. In its place, various types of church-related projects began to appear in the 1980s to alleviate the severe unemployment then beginning to grip former industrial areas of the country. Frequently they were piloted by former Industrial Mission chaplains, themselves now "downsized" along with the workers they had served. As in the United States in this same period, these projects attempted to minister to the material and spiritual needs of the unemployed, and to create training and job opportunities. In the 1990s some of this work evolved into attempts to deal with the broader issues of housing, education, and welfare. Recognizing the need to build broad-based support for these issues, the churches began to organize or participate in interfaith and community partnerships, likewise a direction taken by the religious community in the United States within the past two decades.

The pioneering Industrial Mission efforts of the early postwar decades in Britain, in particular the Sheffield model of Ted Wickham, attracted great interest in the United States. Hugh C. White, an Episcopal priest, adapting Wickham's model, founded the Detroit Industrial Mission in 1956, directing his focus to the automobile industry. Like the French worker-priests and the British Industrial Missioners, White recognized the daunting challenge of comprehending the industrial world, and of responding to it both theologically and programmatically. His first objective, like that of his European predecessors, was to plunge fully into the ethos and culture of Detroit's automobile industry. In this undertaking he was especially fortunate in recruiting to his staff early on two ministers who had only recently been part of a pioneering Presbyterian industrial team ministry experiment launched by the Detroit Presbytery. The two Presbyterian clergy had worked for five years as assembly-line workers at the General Motors Cadillac plant in Detroit, an experience that proved invaluable to the new ecumenical Detroit Industrial Mission (DIM). The Presbyterians' goal had included analyzing the relationship of a particular local parish to the surrounding industrial community, and recommending changes in the church's organizational approach to this new challenge.

DIM's first two years involved the task of establishing conversations and groups with people at managerial, worker, and union levels in the auto industry. Adding staff, which at its height comprised five full-time ministers representing various Protestant denominations as well as a Catholic priest, DIM plunged into its work on several fronts. One project involved the establishment of links between the Mission and four Episcopal parishes in Detroit. The goals were lofty: to draw parishioners into interaction with people in industry, and in particular to reflect together theologically upon the relationship of Christian faith to industrial life. A second goal was that of finding managers, union officials, and workers within the auto industry who could, with training, become in effect the lay missionaries in this new mission field. As in Europe, the aim was not to convert individuals to the Christian faith, nor to exercise a pastoral or prayer ministry. Scott Paradise, an American Episcopal priest and a veteran of four years in Sheffield with Ted Wickham, was the first clergyperson hired by White in the new Detroit mission. Said Paradise: "We needed to find ways to enlist laypeople committed to the task of theological discovery and to form fellowships of men concerned with the meaning and the means of ethical action in industry."[6]

"Ethical action in industry": the radical idea was that the church and its tradition actually had something to say to the economic and industrial structures of society, and that lay church people, drawing upon their own Christian heritage, could be the carriers of these insights in their own industrial workplace. But that goal, involving the commitment of the four Episcopal parishes, proved very difficult to meet. The parishes that had signed on to a relationship with DIM and its work ultimately proved unable to sustain the relationship. Despite their good intentions, the overwhelming preoccupation of the churches with parish life and agenda, and their inability to enter fully into the life of work and industry and relate it to the gospel ended in failure. The challenge of integrating parish churches into the goal of involving them in the life of industry and a mutual exploration of the values of the industrial world and relating them to principles of Christian faith thus remained unmet.

Nonetheless, by the early 1960s other churches and clergy around the country had become attracted to the challenge of White's vision and his bold creation of Detroit Industrial Mission. To explore the relevance of Christian faith to the industrial world of the mid-twentieth century seemed exciting: a cutting-edge experiment. In the 1960s, Industrial Missions were founded in Chicago, Flint, Cicero, and Cincinnati in the Midwest; in Boston, New York (at La Guardia Airport and Wall Street), Newark, Philadelphia, and Washington in the East; in Raleigh-Durham, North Carolina; and in San

Juan, Puerto Rico. As a young invited participant in 1965 to one of DIM's annual conferences aimed at promoting church involvement in Industrial Mission work, I was thrilled and awed to hear the clergy practitioners of this new ministry to modern industrial society confidently interacting with the managers and workers of Detroit's world-class auto industry, and to tour the Ford auto assembly plant in Detroit.

In 1966 Hugh White brought the several missions together to found the National Industrial Mission. The purpose of the new national organization was to share information, collaborate where possible, and strengthen and expand Industrial Missions throughout the United States within the Christian tradition. It seemed like a promising moment, almost a "kairos" moment — the birth of a new ministry to the structures of modern industrial society. Moreover, the different local circumstances in which the various new Industrial Mission project directors found themselves, coupled with their own particular social vision, seemed at the time to validate a variety of approaches to this pioneering work. Here was a new Christian movement, we felt: a movement beginning to relate closely to modern industry, actually gaining access to the sophisticated and complex industrial environment of American industry, its clergy confidently talking the lingo of the industrial shop floor and office.

But within just two years a principal fault line began to emerge within the movement, both within DIM and among the other missions. It was this: Should the work of Industrial Mission be essentially that of a bridge builder, working with a Christian social vision and with applied organizational development tools, to "humanize the workplace" at every level? That was DIM's premise for its work from the beginning. But other Industrial Mission practitioners in the new national network began to feel that the work should recognize some of the deeper contradictions that were beginning to be seen within industrial society, and assume a more adversarial stance: focusing, for instance, on the negative social and environmental effects of industrial development. Scott Paradise found his own perspective changing radically in these years, as his quotation at the beginning of this chapter illustrates. Another minister advocating this latter position put it succinctly in a later national meeting of the projects, "Do we want Industrial Mission merely to grease the wheels of industry, or do we want to challenge the system?"

The wider social backdrop to this intense debate was, of course, the turbulent 1960s in American society: Vietnam, the civil rights movement, a new recognition of extensive poverty in the United States, student protests, and the emergence of the New Left on college campuses and elsewhere. These influences clearly affected the debates beginning about the future direction of the Industrial Mission movement. Moreover, the funding of Industrial Mission by national and regional church jurisdictions, which initially had been generous and very supportive, began to dry up. Alongside the urgency and immediacy of civil rights, poverty, and Vietnam, Industrial Mission — particularly in its attempts to "dialogue with industry" about "deep political and religious questions" — seemed tame and nebulous as to its long-range outcome. Moreover, the ecumenical nature of the projects — for they were ecumenical — had low priority for church funders. Nor was Industrial Mission able to excite funding from local churches.

The effort to build a national Industrial Mission network in the United States had lasted only four years. By the mid-1970s, almost all of the Industrial Missions had closed.

Among the more radical wing of Industrial Missions, neither a vision nor a strategy was yet apparent, with two exceptions. One was the Puerto Rico Industrial Mission, started in 1967, of which I was founder and first executive director. (Chapter 7 explores the work of this mission and its significance for the globalization debate.) The other was a new mission in Boston. In the developing split within DIM, Scott Paradise moved to Boston in 1968 to found the Boston Industrial Mission (BIM), whose goals and programs began to raise fundamental questions about the direction industrial development was taking, with special emphasis upon its impact on the environment. He was joined by Norm Faramelli, an Episcopal priest who brought a commitment to the vision, great breadth of knowledge, and invaluable pragmatic skills. They found an opportunity to raise such questions by focusing on the emerging high-tech sector that began to be established in Boston's outlying communities. They noted that the new high-tech emphasis fed upon the academic research being developed at the Massachusetts Institute of Technology and at Harvard, raising important questions such as the extent to which great universities should lend (or more accurately, sell) their academic and research expertise to the furtherance of an industrial and high-tech system about which fundamental justice questions were already beginning to be raised. BIM's focus also broadened to include issues of housing and transportation. In this it resembled the change of emphasis in Britain in the 1980s to address both urban and industrial issues.

Summing up the whole Industrial Mission effort, what can we say about the engagement of the churches both here and in Europe with the changing world of work in the last fifty years? First, what can be learned from the Industrial Mission experiment that began with the French worker-priests entering the factories of Paris in 1944? We have to marvel at the extraordinary reach of consciousness that the Catholic priests in Paris showed in perceiving that the industrial world of work was a place of profound social alienation, and also that not even that world was beyond the reach of the saving and redeeming action of the incarnate Christ. We also have to marvel that a prelate with the rank of cardinal commissioned these clergy and sent them into the factories with his blessing.

Second, we have to note the great difficulty — in the end, the failure — of Industrial Mission to effectively engage the parishes in its experiments with industry. What are the deeper issues emerging from that failure? While acknowledging that the structures and goals of parish life do have inherent limitations, clearly the education and training of clergy and laypeople in understanding the economic and social structures of the postmodern world and their relation to a Christian perspective need to be greatly amplified. It is noteworthy in this regard that the Presbyterian Church, through the establishment of the Presbyterian Institute for Industrial Relations, saw this need early on and maintained in Chicago for thirty years (from 1945 to 1975) a training program for pastors, seminarians, and laity to study the nature of industrial society and prepare them for engagement at the parish level. Among the mainline Protestant denominations this effort was the strongest witness to the need for the churches to take seriously the complexities of industrial life and their implications for ministry.

Finally, perhaps Britain's Wickham was onto something relevant to today's global realities when for the larger church he advocated the creation of a nongeographical diocese or church structure to address the issues of industrial society with specialized ministries and skills in social analysis, supplied with the resources to sustain it. However feasible his idea of forty years ago may or may not be for today, it does suggest our need for a greatly enlarged vision of how the churches (and today it must be interfaith) can create the structures and the programs necessary to make an effective witness to the global problems of such vast complexity that now confront us.

Perhaps it can be said that even though the Industrial Mission movement greatly underestimated the task of bridging the gap theologically and strategically between church and industry, it was at least beginning to ask the right questions. More important, it tried to respond seriously and with an array of concrete strategies over most of five decades, as opposed to our usual tendency in the churches to create commissions, task forces, and reports, convincing ourselves that we have thus effectively dealt with the issue.

For Reflection and Discussion

1. The Industrial Mission experiments in France, Britain, and the United States seem to have failed in their endeavors to connect the churches to the industrial world. Why did they appear to fail, and what was learned?

2. What are the strengths and the limitations of a church congregation or parish as a place where radical advocacy for economic justice can be practiced?

3. Could or should the churches today undertake similar innovative programs to relate to today's globalization issues? If so, what might they look like?

Chapter Five

Poverty in History I

From the Scriptures through the Medieval Period

Who are [the unjust]? Those who occupy the fields and extract the wealth of the land. Can anyone be more wicked than these men? If you look how they treat the brave but miserable laborers, you will see that they are more cruel than the barbarians....They treat them like asses or mules, or rather like stone, and allow them not a moment's rest.

— St. John Chrysostom, monk and patriarch of Constantinople (d. 407)

Although the liberal *man gives of his own, yet he does so in so far as he takes into consideration the good of his own virtue; while the* just *man gives to another what is his, through consideration of the common good.*

— Thomas Aquinas, *Summa Theologica II-II* (emphasis added)

THE INCREASE IN POVERTY both domestic and worldwide in the last two decades has been amply documented and was noted in chapter 1. The World Bank, confirming global poverty in a study titled *Global Economic Prospects and Developing Countries 2000*, reported that in the last decade of the twentieth century the number of people living in poverty actually increased by almost 100 million. During this period, world income in the aggregate increased by an average of 2.5 percent annually, a stark indication of the growing gap between rich and poor.

But statistics are abstractions, and have little ability to stir the human heart. We talk about "the human face of poverty," but the phrase, however well-intentioned, is seductive, since there is no "face of poverty" other than a human face, a human body, and a human heart. We know this, of course; all our major religious traditions are rooted in the principle that in the eyes of the One Holy God every human being is precious, created in the divine image.

From 1987 to 1996 I was vicar at Immanuel Church, El Monte, in the Los Angeles area, of a congregation which consisted primarily of low-income Latino families. The church had an after-school tutoring program for kids in the neighborhood, and Marta Alemán (not her real name) sent her twin boys aged eleven to the class. Marta was a single mother with five children, living in a run-down apartment complex and receiving welfare. In my efforts to tutor the boys (who were English-speaking) to read, I discovered they could not yet read even simple words, and that although they had normal intelligence, their attention span was at best ten to fifteen minutes. It became clear to me that both their home life and their overcrowded public school classes existed constantly at the edge of chaos, with their mother confronted night and day with how to pay the rent, keep food on the table, clothe her children, and keep her sanity in the disruptive environment of her apartment building, all the time nurturing and encouraging her children with a mother's love. The church had many families like the Alemán family, and to my continuing amazement most of them struggled heroically and even with good humor against overwhelming odds to build a decent family life.

The foregoing is not a particularly dramatic illustration of poverty. But that is precisely the point: it does not need to be "dramatic" because poor families like Marta's are now so commonplace in America, multiplied in millions of stories of African Americans, Latinos, Asian Americans, Native Americans, and also white Americans living in deepening urban and rural poverty in the new millennium.

The prevailing American attitude toward poverty is well-known, namely, that if you can't find a job or can't make it in the world, you have "messed up"; you have not tried hard enough, or you are lazy — a "bum on welfare." Add to this the racist attitude that assumes that people of color are somehow less willing to "take charge of their lives" than whites.

But social attitudes toward poverty and the poor do not remain static or uniform throughout history. They arise out of the social and institutional milieu of their own times, and out of the political assumptions that govern the society. Attitudes toward poverty in the fourth century, for instance, were not the same as in the eleventh century, and neither resembled views of poverty prevailing in the eighteenth or nineteenth centuries. Of particular importance for our inquiry is the stance of the churches toward poverty throughout Christian history. We need to know something of that history so that we might better understand the relationship of such views to the larger historical context in which they were held. In this chapter we take a historical sampling of these perspectives and the response of the churches from biblical times and the early church through the medieval period. The next chapter looks at poverty from the Reformation to modern times.

Poverty in the Bible and the Early Church

It should not be necessary for us to document the biblical foundations for the need of the churches to address poverty as part of the divine commission. Only those disposed toward an ahistorical reading of the Bible as fundamentally a call to the salvation of the individual can ignore the message of social redemption from poverty and oppression that is a foundation stone of both the Old and New Testaments.

It is no accident, for example, that the liberation of God's people from slavery in Egypt through the leadership of Moses is seen as a theological cornerstone by the liberation theologians of Latin America. Reading the book of Exodus and its message — that God pays special attention to the disinherited of God's people — from the context of the extreme poverty of Latin America, these theologians immediately identified the plight of the impoverished masses of their continent with the Israelites of the Exodus event and with other justice themes in the Bible. The many passages of the prophets Isaiah, Jeremiah, Amos, Micah, and other Old Testament prophets, as well as the Psalms, plus Jesus' own proclamation of "good news to the poor" in his inaugural sermon (Luke 4), and Mary's song of God's triumph in the Magnificat (Luke 1) were among those cited at the landmark conference of Catholic bishops at Medellín, Colombia, in 1968. There the church recognized this strong scriptural bias toward the poor, declaring that this indicated God's "Preferential Option for the Poor." Moreover, the Medellín official report, looking at the social, economic, and political structures in Latin America, used the term "institutional violence" to describe the structural injustices existing in these countries. Even though in recent years the Catholic Church has retreated from these affirmations toward a much more accommodationist stance, the positions taken at Medellín have nonetheless continued to inspire segments of all Christian churches, and beyond.

By the fourth century a divergence had occurred in the church regarding the ideal of poverty, namely, the appearance of monastic orders in the Eastern church as a result of the quest for holiness and complete obedience to God; and on the other hand the evolution of a church having to come to terms with its incipient wealth and its recognition by the state. What seems remarkable in the midst of this more "realistic" accommodation of the church to the world is that Eastern church leaders such as Basil and Chrysostom became monks and bishops, holding the two tendencies in creative tension: answering the call to radical monastic obedience while at the same time strongly calling for a just social order. Like Ambrose of Milan in the Western church, they frequently denounced the unjust social order of which they were a part, much to the displeasure of the secular leadership. The social witness of these Greek and Latin monk-bishops of the fourth and fifth centuries was repeatedly cited centuries later by the medieval theologians and canonists as the authority, along with Holy Scripture, for the social vision of the church. Here is an especially stinging challenge to the wealthy from one of Basil's homilies:

> And from whom have you received the goods you now possess? If you answer "from destiny," you are an infidel who refuses to recognize his creator and to give thanks to his benefactor. If you agree that you have received them from God, tell me why they have been given to you. Is God so unjust that he shares out unfairly the things that are necessary for life?[1]

Poverty in the Medieval Period

The social context in which poverty existed in the medieval period was markedly different from that of our own times. Such was the pervasive presence of the Catholic Church throughout Europe in both its ecclesiastical institutions and its theology that it was unmistakably identified with the whole of organized society. This fundamental feature is the distinctive characteristic of the Middle Ages, as contrasted with earlier and later periods of church history. Moreover, despite the abuse and corruption of its wealth and its ecclesiastical power especially in the later medieval period, it consistently presented the kingdom of God as a visible society on earth toward which every human activity both individual and corporate was to be directed. Society was viewed as a spiritual organism, at one with the church and its purposes, the whole of society being the subject of divine redemption. Under this conception, economic activity was only one subordinate aspect of the whole, and the poverty of people was not only an economic issue but a religious issue — witness most prominently the monastic mendicant orders, particularly the Franciscans, as we shall see.

In the past several decades historians have learned a great deal about poverty in the Middle Ages. We need not go into detail here other than to point out the sharp contrast between that period and our own, especially to note the obvious: that the medieval population across Western Europe was about 90 percent rural. Villages of only twenty to thirty families were frequent; the largest medieval cities were not larger than a hundred thousand inhabitants. Agriculture, small scale by our standards, was the main source of wealth and political power. Times of famine or of plenty were dependent upon several factors: the weather most obviously (drought, flood, insect devastation), disease, and most prominently plagues, especially the Black Death in the fourteenth century, which killed an estimated one-third of the population of Europe. Also, wars of varying magnitude between rival princes or feudal lords, and marauding bands, looting and killing for their own enhancement, frequently devastated and impoverished the countryside.

All of these conditions strongly influenced the extent of poverty in a given region. But widespread changes in economic development throughout Europe, specifically the growth of urban trade centers toward the end of the period, caused considerable economic disparities, creating new wealth as well as a new urban poverty in some areas. Even so, the association that our modern world makes between unemployment and poverty would not be applicable to the medieval period; the structures of work and community, and the religious presuppositions and support systems that governed them were vastly different. The theological and practical understandings of our brothers and sisters of that era may thus provide a "distant mirror" for us in the Christian community of the twenty-first century as we attempt to address the new globalization.

Where does one look to find specific evidence of the church's attitude toward poverty in the medieval period? The theologians weighed in prominently on the subject, most notably Thomas Aquinas. Chapter 2 mentioned the two most prominent aspects of the church's addressing of poverty in the Middle Ages, namely, the concepts of the just price and usury. But it is interesting that in medieval canon law — in its detailed and tedious compilations — historians have found extensive documentation of the church's teaching about poverty.

Canon law is the body of law constituted by legitimate ecclesiastical authority for the proper organization and government of the church as a visible society. The medieval canonists — those monks and religious scholars who compiled the various decrees over the centuries into the body of church law — deal with the *external* form of church law; while the theologians are working with the *internal*, i.e., religious and spiritual foundations of church law. But within the last fifty years, church historians looking at this body of law as it pertains to decrees on poverty have found a gold mine of information and insight. Looking at it, we are introduced to a whole system of jurisprudence which dealt in detailed fashion with topics like the legal status of the poor, the nature of their claims on individuals and on society, and the administration of the institutions through which relief was distributed. Furthermore, according to medieval historian Brian Tierney, the medieval church unequivocally claimed the care and protection of the poor in society as being within the purview of the ecclesiastical authority, and thus regulated by ecclesiastical law.[2] Moreover, it is clear that the authority of canon law was acknowledged universally in European medieval society.

It was the untiring labor of Gratian, a monk of Bologna, who in about 1140 produced a systematization of an immense body of writings called the Decretum, which went back almost a thousand years. The texts Gratian compiled on charity and poor relief were often taken from works written in the early Christian era, which in turn were reflections of scriptural authority. In subsequent centuries, ecclesiastical commentators elaborated on Gratian's body of law, creating this enormous textual collection of what today would be called case study law on property and the rights of the poor.

Underlying the texts was the belief that providing material relief to the poor was an act of justice rather than of charity. This belief was much more than a matter of sentimental impulse. It was founded upon the widely accepted medieval understanding of property, especially as it related to the poor and their rights. There is such a thing as a "community of property," said the medieval canonists and theologians. Although private property is affirmed as a right, this concept of a "community of property," having its roots in natural law, prevents private property from having absolute rights. Its limits are seen in the obligation on property holders to share their wealth with those who are truly in need. Such a conviction is repeatedly referred to in the canon law, but it is especially interesting that these juridical texts frequently cite early church theologians such as St. Basil: "The bread that you hold back belongs to the needy, the clothes that you shut away belong to the naked, the money that you bury in the ground is the price of redeeming and freeing the wretched." And even though both the medieval canonists and theologians acknowledged the existence of "idle parasitism" in the community (some would call them freeloaders today), this human condition was never singled out in medieval poor law as one requiring punitive measures. "Poverty is not a kind of crime," as one canonist put it. Thus, canon law in the Middle Ages had as a principal objective the maintenance of the legal rights of the poor in society.

Help for the poor as "an act of justice rather than of charity": this medieval lesson should resonate as a reminder to churches today even as they respond to increasing poverty with food banks, shelters for the homeless, and appeals for contributions to "the poor and needy" at home and abroad. Dr. David Hilfiker is a physician working since 1983 in the poor sections of Washington, D.C. In his work, Hilfiker has come over the years to make a clear distinction between justice and charity. Justice, he says, has to do with fairness, with what people deserve. It results from social structures that guarantee moral rights. Charity has to do with benevolence or generosity. It results from people's good will. But our charity can be withdrawn at any time. It thus becomes important that in our charitable work we in the churches also become advocates for a just distribution of wealth and for the elimination of unjust public policies and structures that perpetuate poverty and powerlessness in the society.

How were the ecclesiastical pronouncements on poverty that appeared in medieval canon law administered? In other words, did they arise mainly out of a sense of charity or of justice? There was unevenness in their application. But Tierney finds that a whole array of technical canonical privileges came to be available to a poor person facing court charges. Moreover, the canonists were concerned to ensure that whenever a person was likely to suffer injustice on account of his poverty the church courts assumed jurisdiction over the secular courts in settling the case.

All this medieval canon law concerning poverty ultimately devolved upon dioceses and parish churches to administer. Although records of such administration are incomplete, Tierney concludes that most parishes — for example, those in thirteenth-century England — had some poor relief funds to distribute. To highlight the diligence of top ecclesiastical authority in administering poor relief, Tierney cites a pronouncement of Bishop Grosseteste of Lincoln in 1250:

The work of pastoral care consists not only in . . . the celebration of masses . . . it consists in the feeding of the hungry, in giving drink to the thirsty, in clothing the naked . . . especially of one's own parishioners, *to whom the temporal goods of the churches belong.*[3]

As the Middle Ages began to draw to a close, changes in the economic and social environment began to gather momentum. Barbara Tuchman, in her 1978 bestseller *A Distant Mirror: The Calamitous Fourteenth Century*, chronicles the decay and increasing dysfunction of both the ecclesiastical and political institutions, and the accompanying poverty and devastation as the period wound down.[4] From the middle of that century on, "the poor law administered by the churches became so relatively ineffective that the secular government became increasingly preoccupied with the problem of poor relief," states Tierney. Nonetheless, Tierney concludes with the striking assertion that "the poor were better looked after in England in the thirteenth century than in any subsequent century."[5]

In that same century, a remarkable religious movement to address poverty began with the conversion of the son of a wealthy cloth merchant in the hill town of Assisi in Italy. It was to spread rapidly across Europe in succeeding decades, strongly challenging the church at the highest levels, including papal authority. Taking literally the words of Matthew's Gospel (19:21), "If you wish to go the whole way, go, sell your possessions and give to the poor," Francis renounced his inherited privileges and wealth and set off for Rome in the year 1210 with a ragtag band of eleven followers. Their intent was to petition the pope for permission to establish a new kind of religious order, one centered upon the ideal of "following the life and poverty of Jesus Christ."

Herewith a caveat. There has long been a tendency in the churches to idealize and romanticize St. Francis, his Franciscan friars, and the ideals they represented, and to ignore the context from which they emerged. It is in fact convenient for us to do so, for we can then point to Francis and his followers as proof that in Christianity we have a group that can totally renounce the world and fully embrace the poor, while we ourselves can explain that we are not "called" to such extreme commitment. In the bargain we can also comfortably adopt Francis's love of nature and the environment, and his love for animals, which serve as justification for the increasingly popular rites of "blessing of the animals" in our churches on or near his saint's day. But Francis and the Franciscans should be of great interest to us who would reclaim our own tradition as it may shed light on a response to the monumental challenge of global poverty and its relationship to the new globalization.

First, some information on the context and shape of the Franciscan movement as it developed. The beginning of the thirteenth century found Western European society increasingly impacted by the rise in trade and commerce, resulting in the unplanned growth of towns and cities. The rise in poverty resulting from the disruption had already begun to upset long-established patterns of rural life. These developments hastened the developing crisis within the Catholic Church, which had long been accustomed to a social order and a morality appropriate to the earlier rural and agricultural age. This change, which according to some historians had begun to appear as early as the tenth century, seemed rightly to the church to highlight the corrosive power of money. Merchants, bankers, entrepreneurs, and other heralds of the emerging "profit economy" began to be viewed with great suspicion. Such was this suspicion that by the eleventh century, in the church's traditional list of the Seven Deadly Sins, avarice had begun to replace pride as the root of all evil.

Into this widespread social unrest comes Francis, son of a wealthy merchant, leading himself and his followers into a radical renunciation of wealth — a renunciation, incidentally, to which the pope gave initial approval. The pope at that time (Innocent III) could see the need for this and other efforts within the church to address these "evils" of society, even as the church as an institution continued to amass fortunes and property for its own power and aggrandizement. Historian R. W. Southern summarizes well Francis's perspective: "Francis saw poverty and wealth as perhaps only a man brought up in the rapid accumulation and sudden destitution of an urban community could see them. He did not have the comfortable sense that all wealth is natural, whether it consists in the command of labor or the fruits of the earth. . . . He could see only that wealth is profit, which men create for themselves; it is something corrupt."[6]

What was the modus operandi, the missionary style, of Francis and his early followers? They were to give up wealth, to move from town to town as poor themselves, to depend totally upon the offerings of those in the locales they visited, and most centrally to identify with the poor. There was something about the simplicity of the friars, their total dependence upon God, and their ability to identify closely with the poor that created an immense response, especially from ordinary laypersons. It undoubtedly helped that Francis himself was never ordained. Only seven years after their visit to Rome for a blessing upon their endeavor they had established provinces in France, Germany, Spain, and the Middle East as well as in Italy. A hundred years later there were fourteen hundred Franciscan houses scattered across the whole of Europe.

There are three insights that the Franciscan example holds for us. The first is that Francis and his followers took cognizance of the new social currents that were developing in society, namely, the rise of what medieval historians call the "money economy" and the accompanying social unrest in the new urban centers (still small by our standards). In this milieu they focused with laserlike precision upon the new poor.

Second, by embracing the ideal of poverty, and by its wide popularity and rapid growth, this new mendicant order of friars constituted a direct challenge to the church hierarchy. Such was the influence and the widespread popularity of the Franciscans and similar orders that the ecclesiastical authorities including the popes were compelled to some extent to recognize their work even as they remained very ambivalent. One is reminded of the not dissimilar reaction seven centuries later by the Catholic Church hierarchy to the Catholic worker-priests of Paris in the 1940s, whose radical mission was directed to the alienated working class, and its decision to shut them down, as the previous chapter reported.

Third, its thorough identification with the poor enabled the Franciscan movement to be a truly authentic voice for them, especially in its early decades — a monumental achievement probably not reached before or since. Perhaps this aspect of the Franciscans' work is the one our own churches most urgently need to find a way to imitate in our own time.

The early Franciscan ideal, even as it spread, began inevitably to become institutionalized, and a split developed in the years after Francis's death in 1226 over issues such as the acquisition of property (which Francis had renounced), lay versus clerical domination, the introduction of a teaching role for the Friars, and a more spiritual versus a more juridical orientation. But despite this split, the Franciscan movement profoundly influenced the medieval church. At the time of its birth it constituted a brand-new movement, one outside the established church structures, and one which has endured, albeit changed, to the present day. Perhaps its extraecclesiastical roots might stimulate us to search for a similarly bold and organized approach, one focused not on the renunciation of wealth but on its concentration, as the latter relates to the proliferation of global and local poverty. In terms of religious organization, it seems clear that such an attempt to organize must in our day be decidedly interfaith, as opposed to merely Christian, and also disposed to work as such in wide coalitions with community and global groups.

As we conclude this chapter on poverty in the Middle Ages and the attitude of the church toward it, it is important to note that the Franciscan movement, albeit the most radical in intent and practice, was far from the only lay religious movement of the age that recognized poverty as a religious concern. We may briefly mention three of the more significant: the Humiliati, originating in Milan sometime after 1170; the Waldensians in Lyon, France, at about the same time; and perhaps more significantly the Beguines, composed of women, originating in the Low Countries about 1216. All three were predominantly lay religious orders, and like the Franciscans, responded spiritually and materially both to increasing urban poverty and the neglect of these realities by the established church.

The Humiliati, who like the Franciscans embraced the ideal of apostolic simplicity in dress and manners, organized themselves in three orders. The members of the third order (all laypersons) engaged in manual labor, focusing upon the poor and downtrodden, feeding them and caring for the sick, giving special attention to lepers. They are reported to have worked in clothmaking and to have supported the cloth makers of Milan against the exploitation of the merchants (a thirteenth-century protest against "sweatshop" conditions). Their members also preached publicly, but because they were laypersons, and because they met in secret, the ecclesiastical authorities generally banned them. At their peak the Humiliati had several hundred houses but a century later they had disappeared.

The beginning of the Waldensians had similarities to St. Francis; its founder was Waldes, a rich merchant of Lyon who had a conversion similar to that of Francis as he contemplated the immense contrast between wealth and poverty in his city. "The ostentatious spending of the thriving upper classes was what made the contrast especially evident...as it contrasted with the urban poor," for example, the dockers and cloth-dyers' assistants who could not afford to buy food.[7] Waldes began preaching the dangers of wealth and the ideal of poverty, encouraging his followers, who included both women and the poor, to preach also. The open preaching, plus the movement's disregard for other ecclesiastical traditions, such as permitting laypeople to celebrate the Eucharist, inevitably incurred condemnation as a heresy, even as it began to spread widely into other parts of France, Spain, northern Italy, and even Germany. In an offshoot of the Waldensians in Italy, the Lombards formed workers' collectives and cooperatives. Violent persecutions followed across southern Europe in the next several decades with up to a hundred followers being burned at the stake. Church history texts usually stress the importance of the Waldensian heresy as an early harbinger of Protestantism in its rejection of papal authority and in Waldes's use of Scriptures translated into Provençal from the church-authorized Latin text. Less attention is paid to the movement's witness to the injustices of poverty, its identification with the poor, and its denunciation of excessive wealth.

The Waldensian movement persisted through the end of the Middle Ages and well into the Protestant Reformation. Surprisingly, a Waldensian church can still be found in the Piedmont area of Italy today. Their regional church body has taken an active stand against the excesses of globalization, holding a conference in 2002 in Turin on this subject.

The Beguines, concentrated in the Low Countries and most prominently in Cologne, Germany, differed substantially from all earlier important movements within the Western church, according to R. W. Southern, in that it was basically a women's movement. It was not simply a feminine appendix to a movement that owed its impetus, direction, and main support to men (as with the Franciscans, for example). Medieval scholars still debate its origins, but the Beguines' movement grew rapidly, appealing to a deep spiritual hunger for a rule of life, and a religious piety and mysticism that was authentic to its members' experience. They lived in houses in small groups and eventually bought dwellings to accommodate fifty or more. They appear to have comprised women from all classes, including the aristocracy and the new merchant classes. "They lived simple lives, gave a promise of chastity, engaged in manual labor to support themselves, set up and worked in hospitals and in leprosaria . . . and had a fairly strict regimen of prayer," according to Mary T. Malone.[8] The records of their existence, still being mined and evaluated, indicate that they began to appear in France, Belgium, Germany, and northern Italy at about the turn of the thirteenth century. There are detailed records of their existence in Cologne, where in that city alone, according to property records, there were an astonishing 169 houses at the end of that century. A century later the movement was in decline, although there are records of Beguine houses existing into the eighteenth century.

Their significance for us perhaps lies in the initiation of a movement by women, meeting women's needs, its appeal to all social classes, and the relation of those needs to the quest for an authentic spiritual life. It coupled that life with a widely imitated lifestyle that essentially renounced excessive wealth and devoted itself to charitable acts. Together with the other mendicant orders examined in this chapter, the Beguines remind us remarkably of a time not unlike our own: Barbara Tuchman's "Distant Mirror." "This twilight of a world headed into decline," wrote Jacques of Vitry, a medieval contemporary and admirer of the Beguines. Writes Mary Malone: "Theirs indeed is a dangerous memory, a memory of a time when the structures of the church became porous for a time... and began to look very fragile."[9]

For Reflection and Discussion

1. Discuss briefly what you think is the prevailing attitude toward poverty today. Contrast it with the medieval attitude toward poverty.

2. "Help for the poor is an act of justice rather than of charity." Discuss this statement and compare it with the quotation from Thomas Aquinas at the head of the chapter. Relate it to the churches' outreach ministries to the hungry and homeless today.

3. What lessons might the churches learn from the Franciscan experience that might be useful to our approaches today regarding globalization?

Chapter Six

Poverty in History II

From the Reformation to the Present Day

Fear not these giants of England, these great men ... that are oppressors of the poor. ... They in Christ [i.e., tenants and poor commoners] are equal with you ... the poorest plowman is in Christ equal with the greatest prince. ...

— Archbishop Hugh Latimer, in a sermon before the king
and his council at Westminster, 1550[1]

In 1638 a Protestant Divine, the Dutchman Claude Saumaise, at last argued in his book On Usury *that interest was now necessary to civilization and that free competition would benefit society by lowering costs.*

— Owen Chadwick, *The Reformation*[2]

Take the working girl, for example, and gather up in imagination the total effect of all the benevolent agencies which exist to help her. ... Measure the force of their reaction on her personality in comparison with that of two economic facts: the wage she receives, and the duration of her working day. On the surface, our sympathies may tinker away pleasantly and our charities may afford relief; in the depths, her life will never be affected until the economic factor be altered.

— Vida Scudder, Episcopalian and social activist, Boston, 1912[3]

IN THIS CHAPTER and the previous one, I am tossing you a fair amount of church history. It may be helpful to remind you why. In both chapters we are looking first for indications of changing theological and social attitudes toward poverty and wealth as the times changed. Second, we are looking at the influence that changing economic and social conditions exercised upon both the beliefs and the actions of the Christian churches. This should offer some important clues not only to positions the churches might take today as we address the issues of globalization, but also to make us aware that religious and historical precedents for our actions may exist. In other words, history is important. As Christians, we have not only the Bible as justification for our economic and social actions, but also our own centuries-long church history, which can offer sometimes astonishing testimony to the issues we face today. So we now consider the period from the Reformation through the twentieth century.

The Reformation

At least two centuries before Martin Luther's break from the Catholic Church in 1517, two powerful historical influences — one within the church, one beyond it — were already beginning to change attitudes toward poverty and poor persons. The first was the erosion of the authority the Catholic Church had commanded during the high medieval period. The second was the increasing influence of commerce and trade throughout Europe upon traditional economic patterns and arrangements at village, town, and city levels. This influence worked to safeguard money and expand profits, thus breaking down centuries-old patterns of exchange and transaction of money and goods at all levels.

For Luther and Calvin themselves, the new Reformation teaching on the believer's direct access to the Bible without the mediating interpretation of ecclesiastical authority did not mean the church could no longer express itself on questions of economic activity and justice toward the poor. But medieval teachings on such broad economic issues as usury and the just price, although given lip service for another hundred years after 1517, began to be ignored. Luther, still retaining much of his medieval outlook, affirmed his support of the Catholic prohibition on usury, but Calvin, who was much more the urbanite than Luther (and therefore more exposed to the new commercialism), lifted the prohibition. The medieval church had cited Deuteronomy 23:19 (You shall not charge interest on loans to another Israelite, interest on money, interest on provisions, interest on anything that is lent) in its ban on charging interest. But in Calvin's view, the biblical law applied only to the polity of the Hebrews and was not intended

to be universal.[4] So although Calvin clearly expected the contract-
ing parties to a business transaction to exercise reason and moral
restraint, the door was being opened to accommodate religious belief
to the inexorable pull of the marketplace.

Moreover, for the new Lutheran and Calvinist churches, the locus
of ecclesiastical authority shifted dramatically from the centralized
Catholic hierarchy in Rome to the larger cities and principalities of
Europe. In these newly Protestant urban centers of Germany and
Switzerland, community committees or consistories came into being,
assuming the duties of administering church discipline, poor relief,
and social welfare. These consistories consisted of a combination of
clergy and elected municipal leaders. In the case of Germany, it was
usually the Christian prince of the region together with leading cler-
ics; in Geneva and other Swiss cities where Calvin's influence was
strong, it was more localized, Geneva serving as the model for other
municipalities.

To our modern ears, this devolution of church authority to a more
local level sounds like a healthy and welcome development. But the
radical decentralization of religious authority, coupled with the new
Protestant assertion that the local body of believers, through access
to the Scriptures, could directly ascertain the will of God, while the-
oretically consistent, was filled on a practical administrative level
with inconsistencies, confusion, and arbitrary judgments. It can be
argued, of course, that in the early decades of the Reformation the
new ecclesiastical arrangements were in practice no worse than the
inconsistencies and judgments of the late medieval Catholic Church.
But as has been said, the resulting arrangements, and the new Protestant doctrine that the believer now had direct access to the Word
of God, moved over time toward an interpretation of Christianity
and the obligations of a believer as being primarily between God and
the believer. A new individualism was being injected into the belief
system of the Christian church — an individualism which to this day
strongly pervades the Christian churches.

How did this new theology begin to permeate the practical outlook of ordinary believers? As is often seen in history, the pioneering

thoughts and insights of new thinkers become distorted or diluted as they trickle down to the practical level. In the case of John Calvin of Geneva, his theological doctrine of the elect derived from his strong emphasis upon the absolute sovereignty of an omniscient God. This omniscient God knows who God's chosen, God's elect, are; each of us is thus "predestined" either to salvation or to condemnation. For Calvin himself, the answer to the question, "Am I of the elect, the chosen?" was known only to God. But as the doctrine filtered downward, believers inevitably began to look within themselves and to their fellow men and women for evidence — the evidence of "good works" — as indication of salvation. As Max Weber put it, in practice this meant that God helps those who help themselves. The followers of Calvin, then, said Weber, create their own salvation, or more correctly, the conviction of it. And if one is seen to be prospering economically, it could be taken as a sign of God's favor: that one is among "the elect" — even though the expectation within church circles would be that such a person also be generous in the giving of alms, and that he or she lead a personal life devoid of profligate spending.[5]

This new theological outlook in Europe did not occur in a vacuum, but rather as the new economic and commercial influences were intensifying, particularly in the urban centers where the new Calvinist outlook flourished. So as time went on, Calvinism, nurtured in the milieu of the new commercial enterprises of Europe and England, began to give enthusiastic endorsement to business enterprise, while the restraining hand of a puritanical and ascetic religious discipline began to diminish.

In his classic short treatise *Christianity and Social Order*, written in 1942, William Temple, perhaps the most socially and politically influential Anglican theologian of the twentieth century (he was archbishop of Canterbury from 1942 to 1944), focuses on the critical change in the Christian church between medieval outlook and practice, and that of the Reformation and afterward. From earliest Christianity to the fullest development of medieval thought, the common tradition held that Christian faith should find expression in relation to economic questions, said Temple. Moreover, the medieval church stood on a firm biblical foundation. "The Reformers repudiated large parts of that tradition in a desire to return from ecclesiastical to biblical authority," asserts Temple. The Reformers found a major focus of that authority in the Ten Commandments. In particular, they found their justification of private property in the Eighth Commandment (Thou shalt not steal), on the ground that a divine prohibition of theft presupposes a divine sanction of property. The medieval biblical teaching, being much broader, said Temple, certainly included the reality and rightness of private property, but it also contained provisions that made the actual rights of property *conditional* rather than absolute.[6]

Thus, as Protestant behavior evolved, including that of the Puritans, it could be seen as moving from a strict and disciplined accountability to God for one's possessions, toward an acceptance of a less restrained acquisition of wealth. This idea became conveniently reinforced as the new capitalist economic doctrines evolved, finding their confirmation two centuries later in Adam Smith's *Enquiry into the Nature and Causes of the Wealth of Nations*, the manifesto of modern capitalism.

Reformation Movements and Voices for the Poor

The first quotation at the head of this chapter ("Fear not these giants ... ") is from one of several confrontative sermons preached by Bishop Hugh Latimer in 1550 which denounced the wealthy landowners of England. Remarkably, this sermon was preached in the presence of the rich and powerful, including the king himself. The landowners' increasing practice of converting plowland to sheep-grazing pasture under the authority of the new enclosure laws was leading to widespread poverty and unemployment among farmer-laborers. Latimer, who along with other prominent Church of England Protestant reformers was burned at the stake as a Protestant heretic five years later, was nonetheless affirming a more medieval tradition in defending the poor against the powerful and greedy.

However, he appears to stand alone among the prominent English Reformers in so strongly acknowledging the social indebtedness of the rich to the poor.

In the previous chapter, we saw the development of religious movements that espoused the ideal of poverty and the cause of the poor in the later Middle Ages. Likewise in the Reformation, a number of new movements arose to continue to hold this concern front and center despite pressures to the contrary both from the churches and society. Conditions in Europe differed from one region to another, but in general the shifting equations of economic power, land ownership, and political control, and the influence of magistrate, prince, or king, worked to the detriment of the poor, including the agrarian poor.

Early and radical Reformation manifestations of what centuries later would be called the "preferential option for the poor" (in the liberation theology of Latin American Catholic theologians in the 1960s) appeared in Germany only a few years after Martin Luther's break with Rome. Different radical Reformers had different emphases, usually addressing themselves both to religious and social reform. As a British historian of this "Radical Reformation" observes: "Even more explicitly economic issues were given a religious dimension: the social effects of a money economy, early capitalist economic practices, the attempts of feudal landlords to extract as much as possible from their tenants, were all condemned as contrary to Christian ethics, as infringements of the norms of justice and brotherhood found in the Bible."[7]

For example, the idea of a "Christian Union" of the peasantry appeared in 1525 in southwest Germany. It was predicated upon a Christian brotherhood, and espoused radical egalitarian social principles encompassing all social classes. The brotherhood required an oath invoking Christian justice, brotherly love, and the Word of God, which was to be taught and preached "purely and clearly." Inspired, and inflamed to occasional violence by fiery Christian rhetoric, the peasants demanded freedom from oppression by landlords, and the restoration to the village community of land once held in common.

The resulting German Peasants' Revolt was put down easily by the princes, but with much peasant bloodshed.[8]

More numerous and more widely dispersed geographically were the Anabaptists, with roots in Switzerland, south Germany, and the Netherlands. They were united doctrinally in their belief in adult baptism and in separating themselves from the world, but diverged in other respects. Noteworthy for our purposes was the belief of some Anabaptists (for example, the Hutterites and the Swiss Brethren) in holding their property in common, based on the early chapters of Acts. An early Hutterite document (1545) denounced private property as "the greatest enemy of love, and the true Christian must render up his will and become free from property if he would be a disciple." Profit was also condemned; no one in the Hutterite community could bequeath property. All that a man used reverted upon his death to the community.[9]

From the Seventeenth Century to the Nineteenth Century

Notwithstanding these and other movements by and for the poor, sixteenth-century Europe began to leave behind the medieval era. As it struggled with the proliferation of Protestant sects and theologies, Europe continued to throw off the remnants of a dying medieval Catholicism. By the seventeenth century, political and social change was overwhelming the hold of the institutional church on its people. Church reform leaders themselves, caught up in the change, generally did not or could not provide the vision to maintain the holistic social perspective the church had espoused until then.

Seventeenth-century England saw a traumatic period of political and theological rebellion as the king (Charles I) was overthrown and beheaded (1649) amid civil war between the Royalists and the Puritans. The resulting conflict afforded brief openings for a variety of religious experiments and opinions, for in addition to fierce and bloody political struggles, there occurred a window of opportunity to question existing religious institutions, particularly the established church, and to envision new expressions of community. As happened in Germany in the previous century, the place of property in the Christian scheme of things was revisited in some places, sometimes radically, especially in a time of human deprivation and starvation, caused both by the dislocations of the civil war and by crop failures.

For example, the Levellers — so named because of their egalitarian principles — promoted political and religious equality. Their more extreme wing, the Diggers, carried this belief to property, the group engaging in scattered occupations of land, dwellings, and even churches. Gerrard Winstanley, a leader of this wing, wrote in 1649 in a pamphlet titled *A Watch-Word to the City of London:* "Freedom is the man that will turn the world upside down, therefore no wonder he hath enemies. . . . True freedom lies in the community of spirit, and community in the earthly treasury [i.e., of land and property], and this is Christ, the true manchild spread abroad in the creation, restoring all things unto himself."[10] Winstanley's ideas embraced a literal acceptance of the communal sharing of possessions as reported in Acts 4. It is interesting that his religious perspective in this passage anticipates an incarnational theology that came to maturity only in the late nineteenth century, one that since has strongly permeated Anglican theology. But the Levellers' rebellion was brief, being brutally put down by Oliver Cromwell in 1651. By the time of the restoration of the monarchy in 1660, this period of creative ferment in England had ended.

In reflecting upon the importance of the seventeenth century in England, and in Europe in general, we should note that the sects on the fringes of Puritanism (the Anabaptists, the Familists, the Levellers, and to some extent the Quakers) frequently affirmed the belief in a kingdom of God upon earth — a view not usually held by mainstream Puritans. Despite their typically apocalyptic and sectarian perspectives, many of these sects maintained a belief in a new social order upon earth, a belief in a society of Christian brotherhood and sisterhood.

After the Restoration, the return to more accustomed arrangements of property and power was solidified, and the English economy strengthened considerably, along with the view that commercial enterprise embodied positive moral values. Indicative of the influence of the new prosperity, and the tendency of the established church to accept and even bless it, an English prelate of the time made the striking observation that "traffic and commerce have given mankind a higher degree than any title of nobility, even that of civility and humanity itself."[11] Throughout Europe in the sixteenth and seventeenth centuries, the royal heads of state steadily consolidated their power, becoming much more efficient and engaging in both local and global trade, the latter now protected by naval power. It was the Age of Mercantilism, and battles for markets, whether economic or naval, were conducted by the state. The church, especially in England, functioned in this new era almost as a kind of "department" of the state, and thus increasingly with a collaborative interest in its prosperity.

The eighteenth century saw a continuation of this stance. Few voices from the churches arose to challenge the social inequities that were resulting from the new capitalist economy. It was a period of religious acquiescence in, and sometimes active approval of, the new economic and social forces — a de facto surrender to the state by the Christian churches of any claim to a moral perspective on economic policy as it pertained to deepening social inequities.

As this century ended in England, the established church showed its indifference to the larger social questions posed by the effects of the Industrial Revolution, particularly the question of the new industrial poor — its clergy being largely aligned with the aristocratic classes while exhibiting a mixture of ignorance, contempt, and fear of the working classes. But as the nineteenth century dawned, the fear grew as the new egalitarian ideals spawned by the French Revolution of 1789 crossed the English Channel and understandably began to awaken consciousness about the social and political disparities of English society. The early decades of the new century saw government repression of widespread social unrest that had arisen in sympathy with the new French expressions of liberty, equality, and fraternity; the passage of the Reform Bill of 1832 (consisting principally of electoral reforms) defused what some historians believe might have been a revolution.

About the middle third of the century, a liturgical and theological rebirth, the Oxford Movement, began within the Church of England. It was a rebirth which gave rise to the Anglo-Catholic movement — a movement liturgically and doctrinally "High Church," but also one exhibiting a renewed social concern for the poor (a development not usually acknowledged even today as one of its distinctive contributions). The establishment of settlement houses for the urban poor by some of the new Anglo-Catholic parishes led to a new appreciation of the depth and extent of poverty in industrial and urban England, and also to an awareness of its deeper causes. At about this time, Friedrich Engels, Marx's close collaborator, wrote *The Condition of the Working Class in England*, based partly upon his own experience as a factory worker in Manchester, a personal experience adding authenticity to his conclusions. Significant new theological and political rebirth ensued within the Church of England, eventually influencing the Episcopal Church in the United States.

Awakening to these injustices afflicting British life, F. D. Maurice (a "broad churchman" not associated with the Anglo-Catholic movement), writing in mid-century, was perhaps the most influential and innovative English theological thinker of the nineteenth century, calling urgent attention to the mission of the church in society. Recognizing the inadequacy of current theologies to address the social inequities of the time, he wrote, "Christ entered into the state of the lowest beggar; our family life, our politics, are all sacred."[12] A Christian socialist, he espoused a universalism in his incarnational theology, which drew much criticism at the time. However, he was somewhat naive and conventional politically, believing the message and good offices of the church, through moral persuasion, could ultimately bring about harmony between the managerial and working classes.

Maurice's fellow churchmen and socialists John M. Ludlow (1821–1911) and Charles Kingsley (1819–75) were more politically aware. But as well-meaning and as influential as they were in their time, all three men approached the poverty of the working classes with tones of class condescension, as well as a belief that the church itself, through its agency as reconciler, could be a primary instrument in bringing about true justice and harmony among the classes.

More radical in his socialism was Stewart Headlam (1847–1924), an Anglo-Catholic who although not a Marxist rejected a belief in class cooperation, stating that the poor must demand their rights and struggle to abolish the class system itself. We should be reminded that the background to these developments in the church at this time were the writings of Marx, Engels, and others on the European continent, espousing social revolution. It was Headlam and former members of his group, the Guild of St. Matthew, who set the tone of Christian socialism in Britain up to the Second World War. Such was the influence of these and other figures in the Church of England that by the turn of the twentieth century it was exhibiting a strong current of Christian socialism among the highest ecclesiastical ranks.[13]

The extent of poverty in nineteenth-century America and the response to it by the churches was briefly explored in chapter 2. It was the increasingly desperate condition of industrial workers in the latter part of that century that finally elicited responses by the churches, and that early in the twentieth century led to the social gospel movement. Two prominent Episcopalians and a Roman Catholic priest deserve mention here as prophets for a vision of economic justice in their century: Vida Scudder, Richard Ely, and John Ryan.

Vida Scudder (the author of the third quotation at the head of this chapter) was an academic, settlement house organizer, labor activist, and Christian mystic rolled into one. A professor of English at Wellesley College beginning in 1887, she and two other women founded settlement houses in New York and Chicago for new immigrant workers. Through that involvement, Scudder came into contact with labor leaders and striking workers in Boston and became active in several labor struggles. She authored several books, and founded the Church League for Industrial Democracy as an expression of her socialist views. As well, she was a serious student and devotee of St. Catherine of Siena and St. Francis of Assisi.[14]

Richard Ely (1854–1943), an economist and author of *Social Aspects of Christianity*, also wrote a widely influential economic textbook, *Outline of Economics*, which sold over a million copies and went through six editions. Regarded as a leading economist of his time, he was a founder of the American Economic Association (1885). While highly critical of the economic doctrine of laissez-faire, he was not a doctrinaire socialist. He favored a pluralist society, one that allowed private ownership in agriculture and competitive industry along with cooperative enterprises and the public ownership of monopolies. He advocated the use of economic power to further the social well-being of all persons, his arguments deriving directly from his understanding of Christianity.[15]

It is interesting to note that although the living wage movement has gained much currency and effectiveness recently in the United States as a response to the steady impoverishment of low-wage workers, a book titled *The Living Wage*, reflecting similar working conditions in 1906, was written by Father John A. Ryan (1869–1945), the best exponent of Catholic social doctrine of his time, according to one appraisal. Ryan's advocacy for workers also extended to new labor legislation to protect workers' rights, and espoused public ownership of public utilities, mines, and forests as well as progressive income and inheritance taxes. His writings came in the context of the birth of the social gospel movement of the early 1900s, and were in turn reflecting the papal encyclical *Rerum Novarum* of Leo XIII (1891), which was highly critical of "the unbridled greed of competitors" and the concentration of the process of production in the hands of a few.[16]

Summing Up:
Poverty, Globalization, and Church History

What can we learn from the historical survey of poverty in this chapter and the preceding one about the Christian churches' response to poverty over its long history that will be helpful to our response to the new globalization? We can see, I think, that the changing dimensions and circumstances of poverty through the centuries, and the changing attitude and response of the churches toward the poor, show that in the first instance the church has been deeply influenced by, and sometimes complicit in, the shape and character of the economic system operative at the time. We saw, for example, that the medieval Catholic Church perceived itself as having a special responsibility to protect the poor as part of the Body of Christ. We saw that that church articulated an economic policy, for example, through Thomas Aquinas's pronouncements on usury and the just price, of economic justice that applied to the whole social fabric, and that the place of the poor in the system was protected through medieval canon law in a comprehensive way. The entire social order, including the making of economic policy, was seen to be within the domain of the church's concern in the Middle Ages.

We saw that in the Reformation this comprehensive vision was shattered, and that despite good intentions on the part of the new Protestant churches, the sharp diminution of ecclesiastical authority in the new churches, together with the rise of a new explicitly capitalist economic order, resulted in the decoupling of economics from religious belief. At the practical level of religious belief, a new Protestant work ethic, having its roots in Calvinist theology, evolved toward a general view of the poor as having a moral character defect. The coming of the Industrial Revolution and the introduction of mass production increased the separation of economics from a religious context, and the churches largely accepted the new economic ethos in spite of the new degradation of workers and the workplace arising from the Industrial Revolution. We saw that no new "ethics of commerce" arose from the churches to supplant the unitary medieval view.

Thus, as the new millennium opens before us as Christians, the conscious or unconscious acquiescence of the Christian churches to the global capitalist economic order continues basically unchallenged. Into our own times, "poverty *is* a kind of crime," and in any case, it is largely deemed not within our purview or moral responsibility as churches to seriously question its root causes.

Yet in our historical survey of poverty we have also heard an insistent voice, one rooted in both biblical and theological conviction, affirming the view that all of life, including economic life, is the subject of the redemptive action of God. That voice, whether coming in some moments from explicitly theological positions taken by top church leadership, or in other moments from groups or movements of Christians exerting their presence at the margins of the church's life, constitutes a strong foundation for a new theological and programmatic response to the new globalization.

For Reflection and Discussion

1. Using the quotation from Vida Scudder at the head of this chapter, discuss it in light of the social programs and attitudes in our churches today.

2. The prohibition of usury that had prevailed in the church began to lessen after the Reformation, until it disappeared. Was this a good thing? Why or why not, and is it relevant to the new global capitalism?

3. What should be the place of "property" in Christian social teaching?

Chapter Seven

Precursors of Globalization

Some Church Engagements Prior to the 1990s

On November 27 the lightning struck. Six hundred members and their families were hit. Three weeks' notice that your livelihood is to be ended. A hell of a Merry Christmas for the steelworkers of Torrance! ... and for thirteen thousand more in sixteen steel mills in different parts of the country. Thousands of men and women who for decades sweated and bled, even died on occasion ... because of corporate greed, we are discarded. Not like human beings with dignity, but like an orange, its juice squeezed out; or even like a piece of toilet paper.

— Pete Razanskas, president, United Steelworkers Union
Local 1414, Torrance, California, 1979

In light of rapidly growing patterns of industrial disinvestment, we ask whether it is not time to explore alternatives to corporate and conglomerate ownership. ... We ask if it is not better to explore new avenues of cooperation and localism in order to avoid the destructive consequences of an economic life that places little value in community. ... We challenge the people in our churches and all people of good will to become champions of afflicted workers and to serve as advocates for the restoration of the control of work to every American community and, indeed, to every community of the world.

— Paul Moore Jr. and John H. Burt, Episcopal bishops of New York
and Ohio, respectively.[1]

MOST OBSERVERS of the phenomenon of the new globalization use the approximate date of 1980 as the beginning of profound new developments in the nature and shape of the global economy. As we have seen, these developments involved among other things a marked expansion of service-oriented industries, a sharply increased shift in American manufacturing facilities to countries overseas where labor costs were much lower, the rise of global financial institutions and banks as facilitators of investment opportunities and capital transfers, and the increasing centrality of supranational trade and monetary organizations such as the International Monetary Fund, the World Bank, and the World Trade Organization (whose precursor in the 1980s and early 1990s was the General Agreement on Trade and Tariffs, known as GATT).

But well before 1980 it had become clear that the power and reach of large corporations in the United States, Europe, and Japan were being extended to Earth's distant corners to a degree not envisioned before the Second World War. Thus, in the 1970s, transnational corporations became the focus of a great deal of discussion.[2] These developments did not yet constitute the full-blown multifaceted transformation the global economy began to experience beginning in the 1980s, but they were precursors.

Remarkably, in the 1970s and early 1980s there were significant engagements by the churches with the effects of an aggressive new corporate expansion, which showed an awareness both of the evolving configurations of economic power, and of the need to develop a response. They may serve us as constructive examples to study and build upon as we proceed later to consider strategies and responses to the globalization of the new millennium. This chapter offers a few examples of such engagements by the churches with corporate economic power from 1970 to about the mid-1980s. They indicate that the church groups involved were beginning to ask some important questions, and were asking them in an emerging new context of globalization. Moreover, they put together strategies through which they attempted to counter what they saw as the destruction of communities, or threats to the well-being of workers and their families as a result of corporate industrial decisions. In looking at these examples we focus on why and how the churches became involved, what strategies and responses they developed, and what wider theological and institutional lessons the church learned from these encounters.

The Campbell Steel Works, Youngstown, Ohio

The closure of the Campbell Steel Works in Youngstown in 1977 was the first of the steel mills to close there, followed shortly by the shutdown of the entire steel industry in that town of about a hundred thousand residents. The impact was sudden and dramatic. Not only were thousands of steelworkers long accustomed to stable and well-paying jobs suddenly terminated, the town itself, overwhelmingly dependent upon its steel industry, went into economic depression.

What had happened? Youngstown Sheet and Tube, a steel corporation in Youngstown, and owner of Campbell, was touted as the eighth-largest steelmaking corporation in the United States. But it had been bought in 1969 by a New Orleans–based shipbuilding conglomerate, the Lykes Corporation. Lykes was clearly not interested in long-term steelmaking in Youngstown. It began to use Sheet and Tube as a "cash cow" — that is, using its highly profitable returns as a source of ready cash for investments elsewhere. But workers gradually began to notice that the ongoing modernization necessary in steelmaking technology everywhere was conspicuously not being undertaken at the Campbell works. In 1977, the Lykes Corporation, its Youngstown "cow" having been milked to the maximum, suddenly closed Campbell, and forty-one hundred workers and their families were cast adrift. The city suffered another devastating blow two years later as U.S. Steel closed its huge plant there. By this time it had become clear that a widespread and deep shift across America in the entire structure of heavy industry, and of its workforce, was under way, and was being acutely felt throughout the Midwest (Michigan, Ohio, and Indiana) and parts of the East (Pennsylvania and West Virginia, for example).

It was the human impact of the closures in Youngstown upon the workers and their families, who were parishioners throughout the city's churches, and the devastation of the local economy that brought church leaders in Ohio together to consider a response. Consisting of both parish clergy and denominational leaders, they forged ties with the local steelworkers union and with the community, obtaining a sizeable grant to develop a proposal for federal assistance to keep the steel mills open. Forming a strong and well-funded "Ecumenical Coalition to Save Mahoning Valley," they sought, among other remedies, federally guaranteed loans from the government to buy the Campbell Works plant and operate it as a community-owned venture. Keeping its primary focus on the well-being of the workers, their families, and the community, the coalition vigorously pursued this objective for over two years. Their proposal generated much enthusiasm and support, and some initial encouragement from the federal government. But Washington ultimately rejected the idea. In the end, at the decision-making level, the view prevailed that safeguarding the interests of corporate capitalism took precedence over people and community.

As the 1980s dawned in the United States, people in other communities across the country began to understand that the collapse of traditional manufacturing was nationwide. The 1982 Labor Day statement by the Episcopal Urban Bishops, from which a quotation appears at the head of this chapter, gave prominent voice to this development, an excerpt of their statement appearing in the *New York Times* editorial pages. In California, for example, the state's huge automobile assembly plants, tire plants, steelmaking plants, and some aerospace plants began to close as production moved offshore. In northern California, Oregon, and Washington, forest products plants went down due to the collapse of the timber industry, creating as much as 50 percent unemployment in some of the lumber towns in those areas. Other regions suffered similar devastation as nationwide unemployment reached 10 percent of the workforce in 1982.

Plant Closure Strategies in California

As happened in the Midwest, so too in the West, workers, community groups, and representatives from the churches began to come together to organize a response. As an organizer in those early discussions held in Los Angeles in 1980, I recall the eerie sight of the huge General Motors automobile assembly plant standing mute in South Gate like an island surrounded by vast stretches of empty asphalt parking lots, formerly chock-full of the cars of its five thousand workers. At our early meetings in the cavernous union hall of United Auto Workers Local 216 next to the plant, we rattled around in the empty space, attracting only ten or fifteen workers, plus a few community organizers and a couple of clergy.

But as with Youngstown, there was also a willingness to organize in Los Angeles. Laid-off workers, community leaders, some aides to state politicians, academics, and religious leaders began to communicate with each other throughout the West and even into Mexico to plan a response. In the fall of 1981 their efforts produced a Western International Conference on Economic Dislocation, which brought together over 550 people from throughout California, Oregon, and Washington, with a heavy contingent from workers and labor union locals throughout the region, including 13 representatives from trade unions in Mexico. The conference had endorsements and financial support from several national religious denominations as well as organized labor, some political figures, and community groups. It issued a "pastoral letter" directed to the religious community throughout the region, detailing its findings and challenging the churches to become involved. A statewide California Coalition Against Plant Shutdowns was formed, which spawned seven plant closure projects in California. The coalition's early objective was to push for a state plant closure bill, whose central feature was the requirement that companies give six months' notice of intent to close a plant. After hearings in the state Capitol, the bill was approved by a committee of the California State Assembly. But it went no further. Some church groups also filed stockholder resolutions with corporations that had closed, or were considering closing plants in the West. None of these prospered at annual stockholder meetings.

In general in California and the West, it must be acknowledged that the regional religious response and involvement had no significant counterpart at the local church level. Thus, in some contrast to Youngstown, there was no concentration of affected workers in the parishes whose presence would have lent more legitimacy to the struggle. Nor was there an attempt, at least in Los Angeles, to activate such a constituency.

Puerto Rico and the Copper Mines

A decade prior to the involvements of these religious coalitions in the Midwest and West, an issue involving a "plant opening" (as opposed to a plant closing) surfaced on the island of Puerto Rico. It involved a proposal by two American-based mining companies to mine copper in the mountains of Puerto Rico. Kennecott Copper and American Metal Climax had jointly approached the Puerto Rican government in the late 1960s with a proposal to exploit rich copper deposits lying in the central mountain range of that small Caribbean island. The open-pit mining operation, to last thirty years, would create a huge hole about a mile wide in close proximity to three small towns. The mining enterprise would itself generate eight hundred jobs, said the two multinational companies, and would also create a new industrial base from which satellite copper industries would subsequently be spawned on the island. It would thus provide major long-range employment opportunities in a country with up to a third of its population impoverished or unemployed, the companies said.

By 1970 the Puerto Rican government appeared close to signing a mining agreement. It seemed to many like a natural and very desirable continuation of Puerto Rico's *Operation Bootstrap*, its highly touted industrial development policy over the previous twenty years. The basis of that policy was to attract U.S. companies to establish job-creating factories on the island by offering enticing economic incentives, the cornerstone of which was corporate tax exemption for periods of up to seventeen years.

Meanwhile, the mining proposal had begun to generate a huge debate in Puerto Rico. The government continued to make no secret of its favorable disposition toward the project. But others began to raise objections. Pointing to the failure of Puerto Rico's several petrochemical complexes to deliver on their earlier promise of creating satellite industries and jobs, they questioned the mining companies' promises of jobs and economic prosperity. Would the poorest and those with the least formal education get the new jobs in the mining operation, or would they be filled mainly from the United States by more technically skilled and educated people? Would the dream of generating satellite copper products industries with more employment opportunities be realized? An equally critical and perhaps even greater question was the mining operation's environmental impact on the fragile ecosystem of that lush and densely populated tropical island. There were huge unanswered questions having to do with air pollution, water pollution, and, for example, where to put the nineteen thousand tons of mining tailings (waste) that would be generated *daily* for the thirty-year life of the mine.

At first glance, the thought that the churches in Puerto Rico might play any role in becoming involved in this issue could understandably be dismissed. In addition to not being seen as a "religious" issue, the mining issue was too huge, too technical, too controversial. But a small ecumenical group in San Juan called Misión Industrial de Puerto Rico began with its staff of two people to investigate the mining proposal. It made contacts with Puerto Rican environmentalists, economists at the University of Puerto Rico, representatives from the mining companies (who were eager to tout the project's benefits), the government, and people living in the proposed area that would be affected. After careful evaluation, and after considerable consultation both on the island and abroad, the mission decided to oppose the mining project and to undertake a campaign against it. As the director of the mission (and an Episcopal priest), it seemed logical to me that the bishop of the Episcopal Diocese of Puerto Rico, the Rt. Rev. Francisco Reus-Froylán, be asked, along with his diocesan council, to take a position of opposition to the proposed mining operation.

The result was twofold. First, the bishop and his diocesan council went on record as opposing the project. This opposition by a small church body in Puerto Rico, although deemed unusual for a church, raised only an eyebrow or two at the time. But a second, more significant action followed a few months later. The Puerto Rican church pressed its relationship with the national Episcopal Church (USA), and the mission worked with the Industrial Mission network in the United States (see chapter 4) to seek support for its stand from the churches in the United States. Those relationships, and the supportive research done by the Episcopal Church nationally, resulted in a crucial discovery: the national church's investment portfolio included its ownership of several million dollars worth of stock in Kennecott Copper and American Metal Climax. Further investigation revealed that five other mainline U.S. Protestant denominations also had investments in the two companies, for a total of about 30 million dollars (still a very small proportion of the two companies' total stock). As a result of this discovery, representatives from those six U.S. religious bodies convened to see how they might be supportive of the concerns of the Puerto Rican churches. They came up with an innovative strategy: instead of immediately joining with the Puerto Rican churches in expressing opposition to the mining venture (for example, through stockholder action, which did occur), they decided to create an ecumenical panel of public inquiry into the issue. The panel journeyed to the island to take testimony in two days of public hearings, which were widely covered in the local press. From environmental scientists, to economists, to residents living in the area to be affects, almost every sector, including the Puerto Rican government, testified at the hearings. The mining companies boycotted them.

The ecumenical panel returned to New York and subsequently issued its findings: the mining operation should not proceed unless and until strong environmental safeguards were guaranteed, and unless the operation could be shown to provide sufficient social and economic benefits to the sectors of Puerto Rican society most needful of them. Public opinion, already influenced by the opposition of advocates for Puerto Rico's political independence, and by a few other strong opposing voices, began to turn significantly against the operation. In the fall of 1971, a little over a year after the mission first became involved, the Puerto Rican government broke off negotiations with the copper companies. To date there has been no copper mined in Puerto Rico.

What were the ingredients of the success of this campaign from the churches' perspective? First, the involved churches in Puerto Rico (not all of them — significantly, the Catholic Church declined to become involved, along with most of the denominational church bodies) looked primarily at the preeminently human and environmental aspects of the mining proposal. In this regard they had their theology right: a view of the whole creation as the object of the divine redemption. Second, the church groups in Puerto Rico understood that thorough economic, environmental, and social investigation was necessary in such a complex issue. Third, the collaboration between the Puerto Rican religious bodies and their mainland U.S. counterparts was integrated and developed as truly a joint venture, not only across borders but ecumenically.

I have gone into more detail on this issue than on the two previous ones in this chapter (in addition, I confess, to my being a principal in this engagement) because in reviewing it I am struck by how much this issue of over thirty years ago resembles issues now confronting us in the new globalization. Corporate power, compliant governments, the insistence upon the validity of traditional Western economic development models as the universal remedy for poverty in all countries: these ingredients still constitute some of the chief roadblocks to a just and humane economic development policy.

In the Philippines,
the Conscientization of a Catholic Nun

Another example of an awakening to the global implications of poverty by the churches in developing countries comes from the Philippines. It is an account of how a Roman Catholic sister there gradually becomes aware of the broader political implications of worker poverty and exploitation, particularly as it affects women workers, and begins to respond.

In 1975 Sister Mary Soledad Pepiñan of the Good Shepherd Sisters came into contact with impoverished Filipino sugar workers and their families on the island of Negros. She and members of her religious order began to respond to the immediate needs of the workers, and in doing so, to understand their abysmal working conditions. When the workers decided to go on strike against the company, the sisters took the decision to stand with them in support. It was a dangerous time: martial law was in effect throughout the country. But the nuns' actions led to the establishment of a "Friends of the Workers" group. How did their actions move to that level of solidarity? "Before we could ever convince the intellect we had to touch the heart," writes Sister Mary.[3] Their awareness of the need to commit to justice instead of only charity had come through their personal acquaintance with workers and their families.

That was the beginning of the Filipino sister's expanded journey to justice, for out of the experience came the need for an education strategy. The sisters began to set up training sessions to develop organizing skills, not only for church personnel on an ecumenical level, but also for grassroots leaders. Three years later she and her order were helping local loggers on Negros Island in understanding their own journey as she led them to ponder and write the history of their struggle. The logging company had withheld their wages for two years, then began to sink the workers into debt for goods obtained at the company canteen. The workers, deciding to strike against the company, nonetheless lacked the support of their own wives, on whom the impact of no income for their families would be immediate and terrifying. Mary Pepiñan and her nuns saw a need they could fulfill: support the women in becoming the breadwinners of the family while their men were on strike. The women found they could extract salt from the sea and barter it for rice. An economic lifeline came into being through the workers' wives and through the sisters' support.

Subsequently, and on a wider front, Sister Mary saw an urgent need to help other workers and their families begin to understand basic socioeconomic factors relevant to their particular situation, and to apply it. Thus began a religious-based biweekly publication to help religious people and workers to put their struggles into a broader social and economic context. In other words, the work began to move the horizons of people from the first stage of simply serving human need, to understanding their own particular issues economically and politically, and spreading outward to the larger economic development issues confronting developing nations.

Such was Mary's own journey that in 1981, six years after her first contact with the sugar workers of Negros, she became the founder and coordinator of the Third World Movement Against the Exploitation of Women.

Infant Formula Promotion in Developing Countries

There was a precursor in the 1970s to the widespread sweatshop protests on college campuses and in churches in the 1990s against the exploitation of workers in poor countries: the campaign against the Nestlé Corporation and others for their indiscriminate promotion of infant formula products in countries in Africa, Latin America, and other developing nations. Sensing lucrative new markets, the Swiss-based Nestlé, Bristol-Myers in the United States, and several other infant formula producers had begun massive advertising and promotional campaigns in these countries to persuade mothers to switch from breast-feeding their babies to the use of infant formula. Using billboards, radio advertising, company-hired "nurses" to visit maternity wards with free samples, and other techniques, the companies put out messages such as this Nestlé radio ad: "When mother's milk is not enough, baby needs a special milk: Lactogen Full Protein." Their core message was simple: the new, modern way for your infant's health is bottle-fed infant formula.

In the early 1970s, studies by various international health organizations began to show a clear negative impact of this infant formula ad blitz on infant health in developing countries. In addition to emphasizing the long-established health advantages in breast-feeding infants, health authorities pointed out that the use of artificial milk formulas presupposes sufficient family income to pay for its regular use, reasonable access to clean water, and access to refrigeration facilities, among other conditions. In the poorest areas such conditions were frequently absent. For example, one study showed that in Egypt and Pakistan, the cost of bottle-feeding babies exceeded 40 percent of minimum wage.

As these findings became widely known, church groups began to take action. The Interfaith Center for Corporate Responsibility, an association in the United States of over a hundred faith-based institutional investors, began to use stockholder resolutions and also to develop dialogue with infant formula producers. The outcome of one resolution filed by one of ICCR's members, the Sisters of the Precious Blood (Roman Catholic), is particularly instructive. As stockholders, the Sisters filed suit against Bristol-Myers for listing inaccurate and incomplete information the company had included in connection with their stockholder resolution against company infant formula practices. The lawsuit went to court, and the judge, while acknowledging the Sisters' claim that the company had made misstatements, ruled in its favor: the nuns had not shown that they and other stockholders were negatively affected by Bristol-Myers's misstatements.

The problem here obviously is the guidelines stipulated by the Securities and Exchange Commission for all stockholder resolutions: while allowing views differing from those of management to be aired, the rules are designed to protect management and stockholder prerogatives. They are not equipped to deal in a substantive or direct way with the social consequences of corporate actions.

Nonetheless, these actions and others by religious and community groups steadily attracted attention to the infant formula debate. In 1977 an international boycott of all Nestlé products was launched, Nestlé being by far the largest promoter of infant formula worldwide. Nestlé fought the boycott aggressively, with publicity campaigns, mass clergy mailings, and expenses-paid invitations to visit company headquarters in Geneva. Despite these efforts, pressure increased against the company, and the boycott attracted wide support among mainline religious bodies in the United States. In the United States, hearings were held in Congress; other countries took even stronger approaches. The World Health Organization weighed in against the tactics of the infant formula companies. Despite all this, however, it was not until 1982 — five years after the Nestlé boycott had begun —

that the company agreed to issue company guidelines to comply with the WHO international health code on infant formula use and promotion. But notwithstanding all this, after the spotlight was off it, Nestlé began to slide back to its previous practices.

Stockholder Action and Corporate Responsibility

In the political and religious ferment of the early 1970s, some national church bodies and religious orders in the United States began to make the connection between their investments as stockholders in large corporations, and the social justice values they purported to advocate as churches. One of the earliest and most public issues involved the presence of General Motors Corporation in South Africa. The central question was whether GM's extensive operations, strategic sales to the South African government, tax payments, and employment practices there were helping to sustain the brutal apartheid system and the white minority government. In 1971 the Episcopal Church boldly made both business history and church history when it filed a stockholder resolution with the corporation to request its withdrawal from South Africa. That very public position, although not initially affecting General Motors operations there, attracted much attention to the new tactic of using church investments to pursue social goals. A year later, several national church bodies came together to pursue such efforts ecumenically, and organized the Interfaith Center for Corporate Responsibility — a step that had grown directly from their collaboration in 1971 in successfully working to halt the copper mining project in Puerto Rico (described earlier in this chapter).[4]

Through the 1970s, as ICCR became an effective instrument for ecumenical coordination of stockholder resolutions, the number of religious groups employing the strategy grew. Issues such as militarism, worker rights, the environment, racism, and plant closures were the subjects of stockholder resolution filings. By the mid-1980s there were over a hundred religious bodies so involved. Moreover, collaboration in filings with secular entities such as union pension funds began to develop. It is also of interest that Roman Catholic participation in ICCR was strong almost from the early years, and that women's Catholic religious orders were at the forefront.

Through the decades since its founding, the Interfaith Center has had its critics from both sides. From the corporate side, the complaint has been that the churches are sometimes too confrontative, or that their research is incomplete or biased. From the religious side, the more radical critique has been that only mild or at best moderate corporate changes toward more just or humane policies have been the result and the overall system was unaffected.

The rules of the Securities and Exchange Commission require that all first-time resolutions must gain at least 3 percent of all shares voted in order to be considered the following year. But Interfaith Center advocates point out that even when church resolutions fail to garner much voting support, they raise awareness of specific larger social issues within the religious community, and also help to shine a public spotlight on unjust corporate practices. In addition, many such resolutions making a strong business case in addition to the social issue being addressed are rallying increasingly large votes.

Moreover, since the first resolutions were filed over thirty years ago, other activities directed toward unjust corporate practices have blossomed, such as boycotts, public policy issue lobbying by churches, religious education programs, and resolutions enacted by national or local church bodies for action on local or other levels. In addition, a development that has clearly been stimulated by the stockholder action movement is the growing phenomenon in recent years of socially responsible investment funds and money managers.

Today, ICCR has grown to include a coalition of 275 Protestant, Roman Catholic, and Jewish institutional investors with a combined portfolio of over $100 billion (but it will be appreciated that this figure still constitutes but a small fraction of total stock investments in the United States). In the proxy season of 2003 at least 140 resolutions were filed with 92 publicly traded companies through the Interfaith Center. Top issues included excessive CEO compensation, global warming, and sexual orientation policies. Significantly, global labor standards for corporations were the subject of 27 resolutions.

Finally, investors with hundreds of billions of invested dollars, such as pension funds from the states of New York and Connecticut, New York City pension funds, social investment mutual funds, some foundations, and some labor unions are co-filing resolutions with ICCR. Some resolutions on social or corporate governance reforms are actually passing with majority votes.

What wider theological and institutional lessons did the churches learn from these involvements? Institutionally, they began to understand that an ecumenical, and ultimately interfaith response to the problems posed was essential. No longer could there be an "Episcopal" or "Methodist" or "Catholic" approach to economic injustice issues of such magnitude and complexity. Second, the very complexity of such issues, as Sister Mary Pepiñan became aware of in the Philippines, demanded new approaches to the education of both the religious constituency and the community, and a new sophistication in the application of this knowledge to concrete religious strategies for justice.

Theologically, the realization (anew!) that the entire globe is the object of divine redemption, and that this redemption involves the restoration of the whole social order — that condition of blessing described by the ancient Hebrew prophets — was one that beckoned, and continues to beckon, all people of faith. It continues to put new pressure on each religious body to evolve its theology toward more ecumenicity while continuing to affirm its core beliefs. Finally, there is a recognition in the examples presented in this chapter that the "stranger within the gate," in the form of the discarded or oppressed worker, the nursing mother and her infant, or the oppression of entire communities, constitute, at least for Christians, the hidden Christ to whom we are called to respond. And in responding, we are, ourselves, lifted up and redeemed.

For Reflection and Discussion

1. In the Youngstown, Ohio, and California plant closures, could church strategies to address them have been different or more effective? Why or why not?

2. With reference to the educational strategies pursued by Sister Mary Pepiñan in the Philippines, how could churches in the United States design similar education strategies at local or regional levels to address globalization issues?

3. Discuss the pros and cons of stockholder action strategies to address current globalization issues.

Chapter Eight

The New Globalization

The Broadening of Church Awareness

We need the understanding and partnership of men and women of good will from the creditor countries. Our destinies are as intimately bound as are the lives of survivors sharing a single lifeboat. Without a global solution based on solidarity, the creditor countries' own welfare can, in the final analysis, also suffer.

— Catholic Bishops' Conference of the Philippines, Manila, 1990

Debt is [seemingly] a necessary by-product of globalization ... just as in Dickens's time it was possible to put people in jail and starve them to death if they didn't pay their debts, so today, instead of having debtors' prisons for people, we have debtor's prison for countries.

— Ann Pettifor, cofounder and director of Jubilee 2000

DURING THE 1980s the United States under Ronald Reagan, and Great Britain under Margaret Thatcher, moved significantly rightward politically as the deindustrialization of both countries proceeded to wrench the social fabric. The previous chapter examined some of the effects of this economic dislocation in the United States, and described some responses by the churches on regional and local levels. Chapter 4 briefly described the effects of plant closures in Britain and their impact on the future of the Industrial Mission movement there from about 1980 onward. These signs of the new globalization of the economic order began to make their impact upon the thinking of church bodies at national and international levels. A new awareness of the interconnected nature of the new world economy, and of the widening global gap between haves and have-nots, began to be reflected in national and international church pronouncements, resolutions, and position papers.

This chapter takes a brief look at some of those statements, which admittedly do not often find reflections in actions at the local church. To close observers of church participation in social justice issues this disconnect is unfortunately not new. National church bodies typically have been considerably more progressive in their social perspectives if not always their actions than local churches or parishes. Still, the statements are significant, and sometimes even strikingly radical in their analyses. We will also look here at a historic initiative in public policy advocacy, namely the campaign to reduce the global indebtedness of the world's poorest countries. It showed that both at higher ecclesiastical levels and grassroots levels, the churches, through their Jubilee 2000 global debt reduction campaigns, could achieve significant results.

Some Church Statements

As early as 1981, the important papal encyclical *Laborem Exercens* (On Human Work) of John Paul II recognized new developments associated with the emerging world economic order: "We are...on the eve of new developments in technological, economic, and political conditions which will influence the world of work and production no less than the Industrial Revolution of the last century," stated the encyclical (section 1.3; see also above, p. 32). In this context, it asserted the primacy of human labor over capital, and affirmed the responsibility of government (as opposed to private entities) as "indirect employer" for employment, and for just labor policies. Other papal statements from 1987 and 1991 urged the reform of world trade and financial systems, the lightening or canceling of debt owed by poor nations, and the simplification of lifestyles in the rich nations.

With the perspective of the seventeen years that followed the pope's encyclical on work, the Anglican Communion, at its 1998 Lambeth Conference of bishops, was identifying the wealthy nations of the West[1] as part of the problem. It was not an accident that many Anglican bishops to the conference were no longer of European or American descent, but were African, Asian, and Latin American, and that their combined church populations now far outnumbered those of the American and English bishops. Said the bishops: "The privatization of significant sections of economic life has meant that ownership and control of major agricultural and production enterprises has been put into the hands of international companies controlled in the West.... Instead of concentrating on the production of food, clothing and shelter for the local community, economies are having to satisfy the needs of international markets. This has increased the division between rich and poor, between the nations, and within nations." In 2003 an Anglican Trade and Policy Task Force was created with church representatives from around the world, its charge being to develop an action plan for the Anglican Communion in response to the challenges to globalization as it relates to trade, poverty, and global debt issues.

Also by the year 2003 the term "neoliberal" was being used in various international church documents to give a political definition to the philosophy that appeared to undergird the new global economic order. It was explicitly defined and condemned in the deliberations of the tenth Assembly of the Lutheran World Federation held in Geneva in July of that year to describe the new global market-oriented philosophy. Said the Lutheran document: "This false ideology [neoliberalism] is grounded on the assumption that the market, built on private property, unrestrained competition, and the centrality of contracts, is the absolute law governing human life, society, and the natural environment. This is idolatry, and leads to the systematic exclusion of those who own no property, the destruction of cultural diversity, the dismantling of fragile democracies and the destruction of the earth."

An interesting sidebar to the pronouncements of these global church bodies — as well as a link with history — is today's small Waldensian Church in Italy. The Waldensians[2] are the denominational descendants of those accused heretics of the Middle Ages who were prophetic witness for the poor. (In seminary, many of us clergy learned that the Waldensians were an early indication of rebellion against the medieval Catholic Church and a harbinger of the Protestant Reformation; there was less emphasis on their strong advocacy for the poor.) At its joint synod in 2001 with the Methodist churches in Italy, this thirty-thousand-member church nonetheless approved a strong document on globalization, deploring "the violent exercise of economic and political power [that] raises to the utmost degree the democratic deficit in our Western countries as well as the Third World," and the ravages of an unrestricted and uncontrolled economy. The Waldensians reaffirmed the need of the churches to deepen their analysis of the effects of economic injustice and urged closer connections with sectors of what it called the "alternative movement."

Moving from the statements of international church bodies to those at home, we see American church bodies reflecting a similar growing awareness of the negative impact upon people and communities — particularly the more vulnerable populations — of the new global economic order. For example, in 1997, the U.S. Conference of Catholic Bishops issued an "International Challenge for U.S. Parishes," under its call to them for global solidarity. "During the last decade, the rapid globalization of markets, communication, and transportation has dramatically drawn the world together. Global economic forces empower some and impoverish many. The gulf between rich and poor nations has widened, and the sense of responsibility toward the world's poor and oppressed has grown weaker," said the statement. It added, "Our nation is deeply affected by economic, political, and social forces around the globe. The effects of these forces are evident in our economy, the immigrants and refugees among us, the threat of terrorism, dynamics of the drug trade, and pressures on workers." The challenge called parishes to become directly involved in addressing these new realities.

Warning like the Lutherans that economic globalization and the free-market system may have become an "idolatry" in American society, the General Synod of the United Church of Christ in 2001 stated that the rules for international commerce of the major international financial institutions such as the World Bank, the International Monetary Fund, the North American Free Trade Agreement, and others have contributed to increases in poverty and environmental degradation in the Third World. A resolution calling for a more just humane direction for economic globalization passed, and called for local churches and conferences to study the implications of an increasingly globalized world for the environment and for human communities. The denomination reiterated this concern at its 2003 Synod with an extensive and detailed pronouncement on globalization, and a call to its member church bodies for political action.

The Presbyterian Church USA at its 2003 General Assembly continued its earlier advocacy of fair trade policies and the restructuring of global assistance programs with the goals of poverty reduction and just and equitable development. With commendable timeliness — a significant meeting of nations on this topic was scheduled to be held in Miami in November of the same year — the Assembly opposed the proposed creation of the Free Trade Area of the Americas in its current form. It called specifically for the U.S. trade representative at the talks to "withdraw from any fuller negotiations on the proposed treaty until there has been full public disclosure of its proposed text, open public debate...and a place at the negotiating table for representatives of the diverse sectors of the civil society who would be affected by this agreement." The Assembly also demanded that workers' rights, human rights, food safety, and environmental standards be included in any agreement.

The United Methodist Church also addressed the emerging global order in a strong resolution passed at its General Conference in 2000. Titled "Economic Justice for a New Millennium," it recognized the rapid concentration of wealth and power by ever fewer corporations and financial institutions, and the growing interconnectedness with national economies, leading to poverty and hunger in the human family. It lamented the realignment of economic forces and structures, and the erosion of worker rights everywhere: "Injustices are imposed upon the people of the world by economies characterized by a concentration of wealth and power, and export-based development, heavy indebtedness, and a militarized national security system." The resolution also strongly advocated environmental justice, calling for economic development characterized by environmental sustainability, and for the simplification of personal lifestyles. It made three action recommendations to all United Methodist churches: inaugurate study programs; work with people in local communities to identify specific economic issues that affect families, communities, and persons (for example, jobs with livable wages and affordable housing); and undertake feasibility studies of nonexploitative and environmentally sustainable alternative economic systems.

In the Evangelical Lutheran Church in America, an advocacy plan proposed for the years 2001–2 endorsed a National Council of Churches policy statement, recognizing that "economic globalization has seemingly taken control of our communities from our hands," leading to the increased marginalization of vast numbers within the human family. Also this church's 1995 churchwide Assembly drew attention to the fact that, measured as a percentage of its gross domestic product, the United States dramatically trails the rest of the industrialized world in providing development assistance to poor countries. It also recognized that global enterprises are increasingly unaccountable to either national or international standards, and called for "just arrangements to regulate the international economy."

In 1994 the Episcopal Church, in its preparation for celebrating the Jubilee Year, and emphasizing the biblical imperative of debt forgiveness, affirmed in its General Convention the international initiatives under way to reduce and cancel debts owed by the world's poorest nations. In 2003, the church's General Convention passed resolutions endorsing the Millennium Development Goals of the United Nations, and challenged all dioceses and congregations to contribute 0.7 percent of their annual budgets toward the creation of an international development fund to assist poor countries. Domestically, the convention passed proposals to urge the establishment of a living wage and health benefits as the standard compensation for all workers, and also recommended that the federal minimum wage be increased to $8.70 an hour from the $5.15 hourly rate.

All of these denominations also identified the AIDS pandemic as an issue related to globalization. They called for massive aid to affected nations, especially in Africa, and also identified the need for transnational pharmaceutical companies to make AIDS-combating drugs widely available at affordable prices.

The World Debt Issue

In 1944, as the Allied nations began to plan for the post–World War II era, their representatives gathered at a historic conference in Bretton Woods, New Hampshire, to take stock of the economic condition of the world. Finance ministers were keenly aware of the social and economic devastation caused by the worldwide depression of the 1930s, and wanted to create postwar policies that would avoid any repetition of that disaster. At Bretton Woods the International Monetary Fund (IMF) was created as a public institution that would address this challenge. It was funded by large grants from the wealthy nations, and these funds were to be used not only to promote economic recovery from the war, but also to promote economic development in poor nations. For those nations newly emerging or about to emerge from their prewar colonial status, the IMF would, when needed, provide loans to stimulate their fragile economies, and be ready to otherwise protect them. At the outset there was thus a belief that collective action at the global level was needed for economic stability — a belief that government intervention was sometimes necessary to regulate the excesses of free-market capitalism.

But over the years the IMF began to change substantially, especially when free-market economic ideologies began to come to the fore in the 1980s in the United States and Britain. The IMF and the World Bank (founded at the same time in 1944) began to see themselves more as promoters of policies grounded in free-market, laissez-faire doctrines. As poverty deepened among poor nations in Africa, Latin America, and Asia, these nations began to need large loans to get a leg up on their fragile economic development. Through the IMF and the World Bank, and also in bilateral agreements between lender and borrower nation, loan agreements began to be signed. But two huge problems became apparent. One was that the size of the loans requested by a country was frequently so enormous that the interest payments exerted impossibly huge burdens — as much as 40 percent of a country's total annual budget — over many years. The other was the provisions under which such loans were being granted. Known as "structural adjustment reforms," these provisions — invariably free-market-type reforms — would require drastic reductions in government social spending in such areas as primary health care, education, welfare programs, and environmental programs as conditions for the loan. Other agreements sometimes included in the loan package required the enactment of government policies which facilitated foreign investment in the borrower nation in situations not always beneficial to it. For the lender, whether the World Bank or a wealthy nation such as the United States or Britain or another European nation, the agreement was a win-win proposition: lucrative long-term loan repayments plus added foreign investment opportunities. For the poor-nation borrower, it was frequently a lose-lose situation — a huge multiyear burden of indebtedness, plus social cutbacks affecting the most vulnerable sectors of the population, steps that sometimes resulted in serious social unrest. These loan conditions were being laid down in a world where over 1 billion people subsisted on an average income of about one dollar a day.

As the accumulating debt burdens of the world's poorest nations became more and more evident in the 1990s, the idea of debt cancellation began to germinate in various places. In England, a group called the Debt Crisis Network had begun in the mid-1990s to do research and to build linkages to people and groups. As the millennium approached, the idea of the biblical Jubilee (Leviticus 25) became the theme for the cancellation of debts. The biblical concept of the Jubilee Year (observed every fifty years) is rooted in the notion of the return of land and property to their original owners; it was seen as a divine safeguard for a just society, and against excessive accumulation of wealth.

By 1998, the "Jubilee 2000" campaign to address global debt had been formed. That year over sixty thousand people came together in Birmingham, England, encircling the meeting place of the G-7 ministers (the finance chiefs of the world's seven wealthiest nations), and called for debt cancellation for the poorest nations. By then, major world religious figures from the pope on down had endorsed the call. The mobilizers of this event, who were stunned by its success, were two large church-related British organizations: Christian Aid and Catholic Action for Overseas Development. Celebrity personalities such as rock star Bono began to work actively for the cause, and even unlikely religious figures such as Billy Graham and Pat Robertson signed on.

Prior to this new strategy to address world poverty, the traditional approach had been to do massive fundraisers focused upon specific areas of poverty in a country or countries. The ultimate inadequacy of that approach was seen in the observation that, although one highly touted campaign had raised $200 million for African relief, this was a sum equivalent to only five days of debt repayments for the African nations as a whole.

By 1999, demonstrations proposing debt relief had occurred in over thirty countries. A petition with over 12 million signatures was handed that year to German chancellor Gerhard Schroeder as he hosted the G-7 Summit leaders in Cologne. The massive public support led to the adoption of the "Cologne Initiative," a commitment by the international community to provide deeper debt relief for more countries, to obligate each creditor government to write off its own bilateral loans to poor countries, and to contribute to a pool of funds to write off multilateral debts, among other measures. Albeit quite modest compared to the needs of the indebted countries, this was breaking new ground.

In the United States meanwhile, a new organization, Jubilee 2000 USA (subsequently Jubilee USA), had begun to mount a campaign with the support of the major Catholic and Protestant denominations. The mainline churches were prominent in this large coalition of denominations, trade unions, and other organizations which staged a strong lobbying effort in Congress. The result was a significant agreement by the U.S. government in October 2000 to commit to a first installment of $435 million for debt relief as part of a total U.S. commitment of $785 million by July 2002. Twenty-six of the world's poorest countries, now designated "Heavily Indebted Poor Countries (HIPC)," most of them in Africa, qualified for debt relief under this new agreement, saving them a total of more than $1.3 billion annually in debt service payments. This commitment by the United States was a breakthrough in getting it to focus on the injustices involved in global debt management. The debt cancellations began to permit some modest redirection of funds to vital social needs in the borrower countries. In Tanzania, for example, they were used to carry costs for grammar school education, costs formerly met through fee payments. Similarly, Honduras was able to offer three more years of free schooling in its education plan.

By mid-2002, however, the debt relief program had provided relief for only one-third of the annual debt payments of the HIPC countries, who continue to pay more than $2 billion annually just to service old debts.

A year later, in May 2003, as the Jubilee campaign continued, a further significant step seemed to have been taken when President Bush, responding to public pressure over the worldwide AIDS pandemic, signed a bill providing $15 billion over a five-year period to address this global crisis. The bill also included less publicized measures to further broaden debt relief assistance to the HIPC countries, for there was a link between the African countries severely impacted by AIDS and those most burdened by international debt, these being mostly the same countries. The passage of the legislation was in great part due to the untiring efforts of a consortium of religious groups working primarily through the Jubilee USA office; the U.S. Catholic Conference of Bishops, the Evangelical Lutheran Church in America, and the Episcopal Church's Office of Government Relations were among those who exerted major lobbying efforts, the backbone of which were heavy e-mail and letter-writing campaigns. In this grassroots effort, said Marie Clarke of the Jubilee USA network, the Jubilee biblical example served as the spiritual anchor for local churches. Clarke cited as one example the Jubilee Congregations program of the Catholic churches. Parishes committing to the program ask parishioners to pray daily for the poor of the world, to write at least one letter a year in advocacy of policies assisting the poor countries, and to contribute a small yearly sum for relief.

Unfortunately, a year later in spring 2004, the president had reneged on the full first-year's installment of the AIDS assistance package. More ominously, under pressure from the big pharmaceutical companies, his administration was resisting the approval of the cheaper generic retroviral drugs to combat AIDS, and throwing up other roadblocks to getting the drugs to the over 6 million people in Africa who need them.

In the joint drafting of the AIDS/Debt Relief bill, church lobbyists and legislative staff, particularly from the U.S. Senate, worked together with great effectiveness — a reminder to us that the time and resources the churches allot to lobbying on such important issues are well spent. But as heartening as these steps of the last few years are in beginning to address global poverty through the strategy of debt relief, it is sobering to contemplate the formidable political obstacles that rise up to thwart and delay. A summary paper of the Jubilee 2000 USA campaign states that even if the United States and other countries strongly press for lower debt repayments, there is still the challenge of persuading the IMF and the World Bank to follow suit. These two entities are still the largest remaining creditors holding the debt of poor nations; they are not subject legally to the new U.S. initiative. And in the fall of 2004, a joint meeting of the International Monetary Fund and the World Bank failed to produce an effective framework for long-term sustainability, despite the admission on the part of the wealthy nations that the present system was failing to reduce the indebtedness of the poor nations. Commenting on these developments, Jubilee USA questioned "whether any debt payments to wealthy nations by an impoverished country grappling with HIV/AIDS, poverty, and disease can truly be sustainable, given the urgency of these crises."

Despite these sobering realities, it is nonetheless encouraging to know that on this issue of debt relief — and we should properly aim at debt *cancellation* rather than relief — the churches have proved themselves effective on two fronts. One, church staff worked at a sophisticated public policy level to help craft and lobby directly for legislation; and two, they have been able to generate strong grass-roots response in communicating with their elected representatives. Reflecting back on the unanticipated appearance of sixty thousand people in Birmingham, England, in 1998 to protest the debt crisis, one is reminded also of the surprise Seattle gave the world in 1999 with its huge protest against the World Trade Organization. Taken together with these recent grassroots lobbying efforts by church folk to reduce the global debt of the world's poorest countries, they provoke a thought: perhaps church people are in fact more ready to hear and respond to the great issues of global injustice than we give them credit for — if only we can together be ingenious, imaginative, and persistent enough to create strategies and opportunities for ongoing engagement.

In July 2005, the eight largest creditor nations (the G-8 countries), led by Great Britain, gathered in Edinburgh, Scotland, to propose major reductions in the indebtedness of poor nations, most notably in Africa. Although agreements were reached to write off about $40 billion in debt owed by eighteen poor countries, and the United States promised to double U.S. aid by 2010, some aid advocates for Third World countries characterized the U.S. commitment as mainly a repackaging of previous commitments and also expressed disappointment that the G-8 countries had not gone far enough.

For Reflection and Discussion

1. Is the term "neoliberal" (used here in the Lutheran World Federation statement and condemned as a "false ideology") familiar to you? Do a search for it on the Internet and discuss its significance (or not) for the churches and globalization.

2. Look at Leviticus 25 in the Old Testament and discuss its significance for a just global society today. Could this "Jubilee" concept be justly called a religious "redistribution of wealth" doctrine in your opinion?

3. How can more churches be persuaded to join the international effort to promote debt cancellation for the world's poorest nations? A suggestion: search "debt cancellation" on the Web sites of the major church denominations to find statements and calls to action.

Chapter Nine

The Working Poor
in the Global Economy
Linchpin to the Globalization Debate

The vast rural peasantry [in Thailand] was being upended, ensnared and eviscerated by the [new] wage economy....A new middle class was gradually emerging, gaining sophistication and wealth. Alongside it, a confused and embittered working class formed, too. The essential transaction in this transformation involved turning rural peasants into cheap industrial labor.

— William Greider, *One World, Ready or Not*[1]

All people know is that they come back to work in the morning and everything is clean.

— Rocio Saenz, 2001, SEIU janitors union official, Boston[2]

The labor of the nation is the life of the nation; is that a commodity to be bought in the cheapest markets and sold in the dearest?

— The Rev. Washington Gladden, 1886,
Congregational minister, Columbus, Ohio[3]

THE FIRST AND SECOND QUOTATIONS above are just two of many snapshots that could be taken to illustrate some of the dramatic changes that have occurred in the worldwide labor force over the last few decades, as the engines of the new global economy churn through our cities and across continents. In the second quotation it is a new labor force that cleans the buildings of Boston (and every other major city in North America), a labor force composed largely of immigrant women janitors who vacuum, dust, polish, clean the bathrooms, and gather the trash left by office workers and managers during the day. Their union, Service Employees International Union Local 258, publishes its worker literature in Spanish, Portuguese, and Haitian Creole

115

in addition to English — a striking illustration of the presence of the new global labor force everywhere. The two groups of working people, one entering as the other is leaving, pass like ships in the night, virtually invisible to each other. The first quote at the head of the chapter, describing a worker transformation repeated in dozens of developing countries across the globe, likewise captures the emergence of a new global poverty alongside a newly created wealth and opulence.

Ironically, it is the third quotation, from an Ohio clergyman speaking out in the late nineteenth century at a time of increasing poverty and oppression among industrial and immigrant workers in the United States — a time strikingly similar to our own times — that jolts us back to first principles in the quest for a moral perspective on the new globalization. "The labor of the nation is the life of the nation." Not the gross national product, nor the amassed capital holdings of the government, nor the index of the stock market, but the talent, labor, and sweat of all working people are the backbone of the nation's life, and by extension the backbone of any truly global society to which we might aspire. It should be the special task of the churches, if they have their theology right, to challenge once again the operating assumption in capitalism, especially the new global capitalism, that this labor is primarily a "commodity," a cost factor, in economic transactions. So we begin this chapter with the plight of the working poor in the global economy, understanding that they are the linchpin in the debate over the new globalization.

In recent years the term "working poor" has come to be used in this country with increasing frequency to describe low-wage workers. It is a salutary development, one probably stemming from the recognition in the last several years that ever larger numbers of people who work full-time still remain poor. Just as important, the term has come to include many people in poverty who are not working; thus, "working poor" can include those persons on welfare. Low-wage jobs in the new global economy are increasingly unstable, both in their duration and in hours per week worked; thus, many persons move on and off the welfare rolls perhaps several times in just a couple of years because of the high volatility of the job market. Moreover, many families whose breadwinner (often a single mother) works full-time at minimum wage cannot survive without welfare assistance. These realities belie the popular stereotyping of people on welfare who are presumed to be indifferent to finding a job. Many studies have shown that the great majority of adults want to work, that they aspire to jobs that pay a living wage — jobs that are not oppressive or dangerous. So the phrase "working poor" is used in the title of this chapter and elsewhere in this book to include all who work, and all who want work but cannot find it.

Why are the working poor the linchpin of the globalization debate? First, they are the primary victims of the emerging forces and policies of the new global economy. It is precisely their human plight, becoming steadily more visible as the twentieth century ended, that began to stir hundreds of thousands of people around the world to take to the streets in protest, beginning with Seattle in 1999. The fact that so many people have been moved to action is clearly one of the most hopeful signs — some would say practically the only hopeful sign — of the new century, a sign that the world has not lost its conscience.

Second, for the worldwide religious community, and particularly for Christian churches around the globe, it is precisely at the human level — the level of workers, their families, and their communities, and their legitimate aspirations to take their rightful place in society — that we are best disposed to respond. This preference does not mean that the other major components of the new globalization such as governments, transnational corporations, and finance capital are not our concern, for they are. Rather, it means that people of faith should approach globalization both intrinsically and strategically through the prism of the situation of the working poor of the world, both at home and abroad. We do this being highly conscious of the intricate relationships that labor — that is, the working poor — has with the other primary components of the globalization phenomenon; and we do our best to bring to bear our passion and our influence with globalization's other aspects.

Workers and Their Jobs

Early in 2004, the mainstream news media and business press began
claiming economic recovery in the United States from the recession of 2001, but the reality was quite otherwise for most working
people. According to the Economic Policy Institute, a highly respected
Washington-based research group, the private sector lost 2.7 million jobs in the two years after March 2001. Most of these jobs
were gained back by early 2005, but almost 7.5 million people remained unemployed, a figure which rises to almost 14 million when
those who have given up looking for work are added. Low-income
single mothers are being hit especially hard, with the nation's shred-
ded safety net largely failing to protect them. Workers' real wages
were declining in 2002–3, constituting the largest wage drop since
1990 — and they continued to decline in 2004 despite the claimed
recovery. But even these depressing statistics do not tell the whole
story. The federal government does not count as unemployed people
who have given up looking for work, nor does it include the un-
deremployed, that is, those part-time workers who want full-time
jobs but can't find them. Thus, the number of unemployed could
be as high as twice the official figures, or higher. Untroubled by
such realities, on better weeks for the stock market the business
pages speak of a strong economy giving jobs a boost; but many
economists doubt that the recovery will see sustained and broad improvement in either the jobs picture or the wage rates of ordinary
workers.

In the wage race to the bottom, farmworkers are among the
most exploited members of the American labor force — a shame-
ful distinction they have kept at least since John Steinbeck wrote
his prize-winning novel *The Grapes of Wrath* (1939) about migrant
farmworkers in California. For example, in 2001 the plight of tomato
pickers in Immokalee, Florida, began to attract national attention as
these workers launched a national boycott of Taco Bell, the national
fast-food chain. The tomatoes they pick are from farms that sell their
produce to Taco Bell. Their piece-rate wages are calculated at forty

to forty-five cents for each thirty-two pound-bucket of tomatoes. Assuming they pick two tons of tomatoes per day, their pay amounts to around $50 a day. The U.S. Labor Department reports farmworker earnings average seventy-five hundred dollars a year, with no benefits, sick leave, vacation pay, or medical insurance. Over the last two decades their wages have actually lost ground. Most shocking, after an investigation, the U.S. Justice Department has found slavery rings of workers to be operating in the fields of South Florida within the past five years. According to the Coalition of Immokalee Workers, the Department has successfully prosecuted five cases of slave labor there.

There are also recent reports from overseas of new lows in worker exploitation, including the use of child slavery (not child labor but child slavery) in Africa. These reports, documented by the United Nations Children's Fund (UNICEF), the U.S. State Department, and the International Labor Organization (ILO), show the extensive use of children on cocoa plantations — a revelation that should stir the consciences of chocolate lovers everywhere, cocoa being the basic ingredient of chocolate.[4] According to Global Exchange, a nonprofit economic research, education, and action organization, the International Institute of Tropical Agriculture reported in an August 2000 study of farms in Ivory Coast, Ghana, Nigeria, and Cameroon that almost 300,000 children are working under hazardous and dangerous conditions on cocoa farms. The IITA reported that 12,500 children working on these farms had no relatives in the area, suggesting they were trafficked as slaves. Desperate parents sell their children to traffickers, counting on them also to send their earnings home. Frequently this does not happen. And overall, the ILO said in a mid-2004 report, about 10 million children worldwide are forced to work in slavelike conditions as domestic servants in private homes.

Thus, in the ongoing pull of workers into the ever-growing urban centers of the world, those left behind on farms and plantations in this new millennium of such seeming promise are frequently sunk in unbelievable conditions of misery and oppression — conditions commonly thought (at least by those of us in the developed world) to have ended well over a century ago.

But the fight to maintain decent wages is not the only struggle workers have had to contend with, for the American worker has experienced other ominous and shocking trends in the last decade or so. One is the dramatic decline in worker safety on the job. Another is an alarming increase in violations of the basic rights of workers as documented by a recent study.

In January 2003 the *New York Times* published an extraordinary series of front-page articles that focused on the egregious safety violations of a huge pipe foundry in Tyler, Texas, and its parent company, McWane Inc. of Birmingham, Alabama. McWane, operating eleven foundries in the United States and employing about five thousand workers, is one of the world's largest makers of cast iron sewer and water pipes. The newspaper's investigative reporters described "a workplace that is part Dickens and part Darwin, a dim, dirty, hellishly hot place where men are regularly disfigured by amputations and burns, where turnover is so high that former convicts are recruited from local prisons."[5] Since 1995, at least forty-six hundred injuries have been recorded at McWane's foundries; nine workers have been killed on the job. Although McWane's worker injury record is extreme, it is indicative of the increasing disregard for worker safety by American companies over the past decade as they press for ever-higher production goals. As a result of the *New York Times* revelations, the McWane corporation is now the target of a federal criminal investigation, and some of its more egregious practices will doubtless be eliminated. But in general, the fines of government safety inspectors invariably amount to a token slap on the wrist, being easily paid while safety and labor violations continue, and no prison sentences result. The violations continue because the penalties for safety violations under current law are far too insignificant to be a deterrent, and because the number of inspectors in the federal Occupational Safety and Health Administration is totally inadequate to properly police the workplace for safety.

Regarding basic rights of workers on the job, the recognized cornerstone of such rights worldwide since it first appeared in late-eighteenth-century England is the right of freedom of association in the workplace. Labor laws of nations the world over, including the United States, have inscribed this right in law. In practice, however, this fundamental right — never having attained full practical effect — is today being badly undermined. The widely respected organization Human Rights Watch, in a study titled "Unfair Advantage" and completed after extensive research and interviews around the United States, found widespread labor rights violations under internationally recognized human rights standards. In congressional testimony presented in June 2002, the organization found that "freedom of association is a right under severe, often buckling pressure when workers try to exercise it." It found that U.S. labor law is feebly enforced and filled with loopholes, and documentation by the National Labor Relations Board showed that reprisals against workers who tried to exercise their rights to organize grew from cases numbering in the hundreds in the 1950s to around twenty-four thousand in 1998.[6]

Coupled with this trend is companies' increasing use of "labor relations consultants" to assist them in maintaining a union-free environment (organized labor's term for these consultants is "union busters"). These consultants, highly paid and expert in the niceties of labor law, are frequently very effective, their Web sites openly touting their successes in defeating union drives. In the Los Angeles area in the period from 1999 to 2001, Catholic HealthCare West, owner of a string of Catholic hospitals, and Good Samaritan Hospital, founded by the Episcopal Church, both employed such firms to defeat union drives, despite strong protests by both Catholic and Episcopal clergy, who supported hospital nurses and other workers. Happily, both hospital groups ultimately signed union agreements. Unfortunately, such outcomes across the nation are substantially different.

Trade Unions and Worker Justice

Why unions? Unfortunately, even in progressive religious circles there is a surprising lack of understanding not only of the place of trade

unions as instruments of social justice, but of the central contributions they have made historically, not only to union members, but to
the well-being of all working people in the United States. It was not,
for example, Franklin Roosevelt who first conceived of enacting key
reforms for working people; it was the leadership of organized labor
and its members who fought for labor reforms and pressured the
federal government to enact them into law. For example, the eight-
hour day, prohibitions on child labor, Social Security, the minimum
wage, pensions, and laws supporting the right to organize (such as the
Wagner Act of 1935): all these reforms and more became accepted
features of American life because the decades-long push of organized
labor made them happen. Such worker protections are under strong
attack today not only in the United States but worldwide in the belief
that free-market ideology and the liberalization of trade must prevail
if we are to have global prosperity — unions constituting an imped-
iment to such goals. It is, of course, the world's lower-paid workers
who will be wearing the "Golden Straitjacket" — that is, suffering
the austerity measures suggested for the developing countries by *New
York Times* foreign affairs columnist Thomas Friedman in order for
the new global prosperity to work.[7]

The American labor movement has had its downsides in our history. In the 1950s and '60s and into the '70s, "big labor" seemed
prosperous and somewhat arrogant. "Business unionism," a label
describing the cozy and mutually advantageous relationship between
business and labor, keeping both prosperous and happy, was widely
practiced. Moreover, as the civil rights struggles of the 1960s gained
strength, the labor movement as a whole did not commit its organizational power to this historic justice issue, even though African
American workers would have benefited immeasurably from its support. One significant exception to this was the stance of the United
Auto Workers, whose president, Walter Reuther, strongly supported
racial equality, standing consistently alongside Martin Luther King Jr.
in the struggles of these years. Reuther was a giant in the labor movement and a tireless advocate for working people everywhere. But most

unions in the sixties continued to have racist and discriminatory practices, a condition which, although markedly improved today, has not yet been fully eradicated.

In those decades of the Cold War, the national leadership of the AFL-CIO also became obsessed with pursuing an international anticommunist strategy, a strategy which included not only undercover collaboration with the CIA, but also a collaboration with the Reagan administration's attempted suppression of progressive labor movements in Central America and elsewhere. This doctrinaire anticommunist stance also inhibited the more progressive elements of the labor movement domestically. A notable exception was the International Longshore and Warehouse Union (ILWU). Definitively shaped by the strong and visionary leadership of Harry Bridges over many years, the ILWU, in contrast to the AFL-CIO's position, maintained its progressive internationalist outlook in solidarity with dockworkers and longshoremen and women around the world. During the apartheid years of the South African regime, for example, ILWU members refused to handle cargo destined for that country. In its May 2003 convention, ILWU members voted to support trade unionists in Colombia in their call for an international boycott of Coca-Cola for its brutal suppression of workers' rights to organize there, deciding also to remove Coke vending machines from its union halls in America.

During these decades, the primary union goal of organizing the unorganized wherever they were to be found mostly fell by the wayside. Union membership has fallen from a high of 35 percent of the workforce after World War II to about 12 percent today.

By 1995, however, positive changes in union leadership at the top began to occur. John Sweeney was elected president of the AFL-CIO, and the emphasis began to shift markedly again toward organizing as a primary goal. At other levels of the labor movement, people of color began to occupy more key leadership positions. The unions also began to understand that low-wage immigrants, whether documented or undocumented, were both highly vulnerable to employer exploitation, and also capable of assuming active and militant leadership roles in the labor movement. This very significant change became most evident in Southern California. As we shall see in chapter 12, this change provided crucial opportunities for close collaboration between the interfaith religious community and the "new" labor movement there.

Today, labor faces major challenges in furthering its own organizing goals, in its legislative advocacy for workers in a time of government policies overwhelmingly weighted toward business and corporations, and in the push by the advocates of global capitalism for free trade, free markets, and government deregulation. In July 2005, several large member unions of the AFL-CIO, concerned about the continuing decline in organizing, pulled out of the labor federation.

If the American labor movement today faces great challenges, even more daunting is the situation for organized labor in developing countries. Labor movements at their best have posed a countervailing power to corporate power. But in the collaborative international arrangements that characterize the new globalization, transnational corporations, international financial institutions, and international trade groups such as the World Trade Organization pose unprecedented challenges to labor movements accustomed to working only within their national borders. It is the mobility of production facilities, and the centralization of decision making, that modern logistics and technology have so greatly simplified that threatens the stability and integrity of the worldwide workforce. For example, if a corporation with factory operations in several countries encounters unfavorable labor conditions in one country, it may transfer production to another of its factories, or open a factory in a new country, one willing and eager to accommodate its desires.

Trade unions around the world have recognized these realities for a number of years, and have sought ways to respond. It was a very positive sign that workers came from all over the world to Seattle to protest the 1999 meeting of the World Trade Organization with precisely such concerns. But many years prior to Seattle, organizations such as the United Nations–related International Labor Organization (ILO) have provided valuable research and assistance to workers, unions, and governments. The ILO formulates and reviews international labor standards and provides educational and technical assistance to countries on the right of free association, the right to organize, employer-employee relations, and other areas of concern. It also conducts international campaigns to promote labor rights, such as its current campaign to eliminate child labor around the world. Over 132 nations have ratified an agreement against the worst abuses of child labor, such as the use of children in slavery or near-slavery working conditions.

The record of exploitation, violence, and repression directed against workers in developing nations is tragically long. In Nigeria, Indonesia, and Colombia, for example, trade unionists are frequently in physical danger for their union activities. In Colombia, 135 trade unionists were murdered in one recent year, some of them in attempts to organize Coca-Cola plants, as mentioned above. According to the ILO, the use of child labor is growing in industries whose products are sold in world markets, and could now be as much as 5 percent of the total labor force working in such export industries. The carpet-making industry is one such industry high in its use of child labor.

Religion and Labor in America: There Is a History

In the last quarter of the nineteenth century, the rise of massive poverty and exploitation in the workplace coupled with the brutal and violent repression of striking workers began finally to stir the social conscience of significant numbers of churches and church leadership. The glaring concentration of corporate wealth and influence into fewer and fewer hands underlined the extreme disparity. Coupled with widespread unemployment, the desperate plight of coal miners, railroad workers, and steelworkers began to weigh more heavily on the consciences of some clergy and religious leaders than did the traditional Protestant values of hard work, obedience to authority, and personal moral rectitude — core values of the American work

ethic. An influential church periodical, *The Congregationalist*, captured the beginning of the shift in 1883: "The days are gone in which
these organizations [i.e., trade unions] were regarded by the general
public as well as by capitalists in particular, as wholly evil."[8] This
backhanded endorsement of unions gained strength as conditions
for workers worsened. By 1886, for example, the Women's Christian Temperance Union, led by Frances E. Willard, had sent a letter
to "all Knights of Labor, Trade Unions, and other Labor Organizations," pledging to work for "cooperation, arbitration of disputes,
and the elevation of women."[9] In the two decades from 1890 to 1910,
church support grew considerably for organized labor's aims, and for
the wider goals of working people such as the living wage and the
eight-hour day.

We could hardly write about religion and labor without mention-
ing two towering religious figures in the twentieth century, both of
them Roman Catholic: Dorothy Day and Monsignor George Higgins. Taken together, their influence ranged from the 1930s to the
end of the century. Dorothy Day, founder of the Catholic Worker
Movement, became widely known as a writer through the *Catholic
Worker*, the newspaper she founded in the early 1930s. Her columns
in this pennies-cheap weekly paper, dedicated to lifting up the plight
of the working poor and the homeless in the desperate Depression
years of the 1930s, became highly influential not only among religious readers but far beyond. Hospitality for the poor was also a
trademark of Day's philosophy; there were thirty-six Catholic Worker
houses founded by 1936 around the country as hospitality centers.
Although it was primarily through her writings and her numerous ap-
pearances that she addressed crucial issues affecting workers and the
poor, she did not hesitate to inject herself into specific controversies
or to go to jail. In 1936, for example, when the automobile workers in Flint, Michigan, were engaged in a history-making weeks-long
sit-down strike for recognition of their union, Dorothy Day came
personally to encourage them. Another moving act of solidarity was
with the farmworkers in California, where she joined César Chavez
on the picket line, and although at age seventy-six she was now in

very frail health, she was jailed for several days for nonviolent civil disobedience. She was also highly articulate in defense of the civil rights movement of the 1960s, participating in several events. Her critique of the abuses that industrial capitalism inflicted upon workers was trenchant. Overall, Dorothy Day's life and writings pushed the Catholic Church to pay heed to its best and deepest traditions of upholding social justice for the working poor during a century of "industrial progress" that tended to regard the poor as expendable. The forcefulness of her social conscience carried its influence far beyond the confines of her church. She died in 1980.

It was Monsignor George Higgins who was known throughout the Catholic Church and beyond it as "Labor's Priest." Shortly after his death in 2002 at the age of eighty-six, the executive council of the AFL-CIO paid him high tribute, calling him "the twentieth century's leading advocate of a religion-labor alliance."

His close interest in and involvement with working people and the labor movement were characterized by his strong moral witness for workers whenever their dignity was denied, their rights were suppressed, or they were beaten or harassed. "He was consistently, forthrightly and courageously the advocate for farmworkers, auto workers and hospital workers" among many others, said the labor federation, not just by writing or speaking on their behalf but by being physically present with them in their particular struggles.[10]

He was highly influential, for example, in the farmworkers' struggles in California and was constantly present alongside them and union leader Chavez. Higgins was also a staunch advocate early on for better relations between Catholics and Jews, especially in their joint interest in justice in the workplace.

A third figure, less well known but having lasting influence in both the Methodist Church and beyond it, was Willard Uphaus, founder of the National Religion and Labor Foundation (RLF) in 1932. Its founding manifesto included the names of nationally prominent Methodist, Catholic, and Jewish leaders, and the organization involved a broad spectrum of religious and union leaders, including board members Reinhold Niebuhr and Harry F. Ward. In its first few years the RLF focused on supporting the emergence of industrial unions. But from the beginning, it was also intensely involved with southern agricultural labor, and inevitably with the racism that was endemic to that sector. In its work, the RLF was unstintingly racially inclusive; Uphaus himself, this early on in the United States, was closely associated with early Christian movements for racial and economic justice in the South, including the Southern Tenant Farmers Union and the Highlander Folk School in Tennessee. But the RLF also developed work with theological students on about fifteen seminary campuses to introduce students to worker justice issues. In the organization's peak year, 1947, it also could count twenty-seven religion and labor groups scattered around the country. Not surprisingly, for a religious-based group to be closely involved with labor unions in these decades, plus be racially inclusive in its work and outlook, was to be accused of being communist, and Uphaus and his group were no exception. The RLF continued its work until 1951, when Uphaus resigned over internal disagreements regarding the direction of the group.

Beginning in the 1960s, the drive headed by César Chavez to unionize farmworkers began to pull in nationwide religious support, both on the picket line and in marches, and also in the effective boycott of grapes and Gallo wine made by producers who were resisting the workers' drive for a union. The original push for a union had come from Filipino farmworkers who invited their Mexican fellow-workers into their union, attracting Chavez's attention. The movement soon expanded to include the more numerous farmworkers of Mexican descent. The National Farmworker Ministry, organized in these years, became a very effective voice through which the religious community became engaged across the country, even though the issue of open church support of a union still stirred strong opposition. Chavez, himself a devout Catholic, helped imbue the farmworker movement with a strong religious cast. This marked participation of the religious community in a union cause in the 1960s and 1970s was the most visible labor cause in an otherwise mostly dormant religion-labor landscape until the mid-1990s. But by then the increasing gap between rich and poor and the increasing vulnera-bility of the working poor to severe exploitation were again becoming visible to the religious community even as they had a century before, as well as in the turbulent 1930s.

Chapter 12 explores the emergence of this new religious support for workers and examines its significance for involvement in the issues of the new globalization. First we turn to look more closely at the big picture: the daunting realities of the new "Global Household," that is, the new global economy; and the perspective that a renewed appreciation of a Christian global theology might bring to it.

For Reflection and Discussion

1. What groups of workers in your community would you identify as the "working poor"? Are any of the working poor members of your church?

2. Can you identify a specific issue in your community that is criti-cal for workers? If not, what about workers in other parts of the country or the world? How might your church become engaged?

3. Should freedom of association (the right to organize) in the workplace be regarded as a basic human right? Why or why not?

Chapter Ten

Oikonomia and the Global Household
Lazarus at the Gates of the Mansion[1]

The World Is Ten Years Old

It was born when the [Berlin] wall fell in 1989.... Many world markets are only recently freed, governed for the first time by the emotions of the people rather than the fists of the state.... The spread of free markets and democracy around the world is permitting more people everywhere to turn their aspirations into achievements....

— From a full-page ad placed by Merrill Lynch in major newspapers
around the United States, October 11, 1998

Alabanza

Alabanza. Praise Manhattan from 107 flights up like Atlantis glimpsed through the windows of an ancient aquarium, praise the great windows where immigrants from the kitchen could squint and almost see their world, hear the chant of nations Ecuador, Mexico, República Dominicana, Haiti, Yemen, Ghana, Bangladesh alabanza. Praise the kitchen in the morning where the gas burned blue on every stove and exhaust fans fired the diminutive propellers, hands cracked eggs with quick thumbs or sliced open cartons to build an altar of cans — alabanza. Praise the busboys' music, the chime, chime of his dishes and silverware in the tub — alabanza.... When the war began from Manhattan and Kabul two constellations of smoke rose and drifted to each other mingling in icy air....

— From "Alabanza: In Praise of Local 100," by Martin Espada, dedicated
to the memory of the workers in the Windows of the World restaurant
at the top of one of the World Trade Center Towers on September 11, 2001.
Alabanza means "praise" in Spanish.

When Jesus came to Nazareth, where he had been brought up, he went to the synagogue on the sabbath day, as was his custom. He stood up to read, and the scroll of the prophet Isaiah was given to him: "The spirit of the Lord is upon me, because he has anointed me to bring good news to the poor. He has sent me to proclaim release to the captives and recovery of sight to the blind, to let the oppressed go free, to proclaim the year of the Lord's favor."

— Luke 4:16, 18–19, NRSV

T HE QUOTATIONS on the preceding page offer three versions of the dream of a new world to come.

How is the economy doing? That question daily commands the rapt attention of businesses, investors, traders, government planners, politicians, and others the world over. Every flutter, every projection, every surge or slump in the configuration of the numbers and statistics that reflect the state of "the economy" is scrutinized with the attention a doctor or nurse gives to the systolic and diastolic numbers of a patient's blood pressure. For two hundred years and more, it has been thus in the Western world. Such attentiveness is of course warranted, because it is understood by everyone that when we speak of the economy today we are dealing with a critical reality: the production, distribution, and consumption of goods and services of a nation, a region or city, or the globe.

But the word "economy" did not always have this particular use. Its current definition has been strongly shaped by the evolution of capitalism in the eighteenth century with the publication of Adam Smith's *The Wealth of Nations* and the onset of the Industrial Revolution. The Greek root of the word is *oikonomia*, itself a composite of two other Greek words: *oikos*, house, and *nomos*, from the Greek *nemein*, to manage or control. Thus, according to the Oxford English Dictionary, one definition of economy is "The art or science of managing a household."

And interestingly, prior to the eighteenth century, the word also had a theological meaning: "The method of the divine government of the world."[2] These root meanings suggest a much more comprehensive understanding of what we are about when we address the issue of global economic justice. To speak about the economy in this way means to think about the global household: the well-being of the whole human community. It is to understand that a truly globalizing economy should not be thought of as an end in itself, but rather as a means to ensure that all members of this household are included under one roof, able to share equitably in the fruits and labor of the earth.

This critical insight gives our own Christian social tradition, interpreted at its best, an opening to evaluate all economic traditions and the values that underlie them. To look at our evolving tradition alongside the evolution of economic theory and practice up to and including the new global economic order, I chose three themes in this book through which that relationship might be glimpsed. In chapter 3 I explored work and its evolution, and in chapters 5 and 6, changing concepts of poverty. In this chapter I look at the third of these themes: *oikonomia*, the Global Household. With this third theme I step back to give an overview of globalization, new millennium–style, and then compare it with a Christian global vision, one deeply rooted in our own religious history.

What are some of the dynamics we need to understand about the global economy? What are some of the principal highlights or landmarks of the current global landscape? What political and ideological assumptions appear to underlie this global transformation in the last two or three decades? And how might we see all of this through the prism of a Christian worldview?

"Money Makes the World Go Around"

Globalization, new millennium-style. As previously noted, one of its most salient characteristics is the radically increased versatility of money. Not only has money metamorphosed on the world scene from "greenbacks" into electronic gigabytes (vastly increasing the volume of transactions), it has increased its ability to attach or detach itself instantaneously to or from other monetary gigabytes, doing it in increasingly complex ways — ways not well understood but by a relatively few financial specialists, and sometimes not even these.

Taking note of these new complexities, Barbara Garson, a playwright and investigative journalist, embarked upon a novel idea back in 1994. She set out literally to track her modest investments through their travels in the global economy. Investing $29,500 in her local bank in Millbrook, New York, and a subsequent smaller investment in a mutual fund, she traces where her money actually goes by interviewing bankers, investors, traders, and others along its routes. She eventually travels to see some of her money ending up at a shrimp farm in Malaysia, another bit of it indirectly going to street vendors outside the barricaded gates of an oil refinery in Thailand, and yet a third part of it ending up assisting in the purchase and subsequent massive downsizing of the bankrupt Sunbeam Corporation, and the loss of many stable and well-paying jobs.[3]

Garson's story is a striking parable through which to see a major aspect of the new global economy at work. She takes us step by step as we see her money invested, combined, converted to a letter of credit, and zipped electronically across the globe. She discovers that her money is not primarily used for building new factories or other job-creating enterprises offering decent wages to previously impoverished workers, but rather that, along with the investments of others, it is basically employed along the way in gaining lucrative profits for those who handle her money. In the case of the Malaysian shrimp farmers, they make decent pay as workers, but the shrimp farming enterprise itself is discovered to be highly polluting of coastal waters and a long-term health hazard to its workers.

How did the use of money to make money gain ascendancy over the use of money to invest in factories to produce a product and employ people? A glance at the early postwar decades is revealing. In the 1960s the postwar economies of Japan and Europe, newly rebuilt after their devastation in World War II, began to gain ground on U.S. economic superiority. In the decade 1960–70, for example, the U.S. share of total world trade declined by 16 percent. Another indicator of the loss of economic ground to Europe and Japan showed a sharp drop in the number of the world's largest transnational corporations (TNCs) based in the United States: in 1959, 111 of 156 TNCs worldwide had U.S. headquarters, but by 1976 that number had dropped to 68. For American economic planners, these and other developments represented a serious challenge to the relentless need of the capitalist engine to expand. It precipitated an urgent search for new policies to stem the decline.

In 1971, as international confidence in the dollar weakened, the United States went off the gold standard that had linked the dollar's value to gold as the accepted standard of value among the trading nations of the world. This decoupling of currencies to gold meant that henceforth the dollar and other world currencies could fall or rise in value according to the demand for them on the currency market. Thus, as Kevin Phillips points out, fixing the value of currencies passed in practice to the financial centers of the world, where speculation could abound, and huge sums be garnered. As time passed, "the interaction of economic volatility and billions of dollars' worth of computers, programmed by the country's best mathematical and financial minds put the nation's leading financial organizations into a catbird seat," writes Phillips.[4] The answer to the crisis in American economic primacy was a new economic strategy: emphasize cash management and its profitability over the traditional commitment to manufacture a product. An early prime example of this new strategy was the decision by the Lykes Corporation, the new owner of Youngstown Sheet and Tube in Ohio, to use that steel company for a few years as a "cash cow," milking it for high profits that provided capital for investment elsewhere, then closing it in 1977. The ecumenical coalition that was combating the closure found itself powerless to combat this new tactic.[5]

Globalization and Technology Advances

Leaps in science and technology, most prominently in transportation and communication, constitute a second major dynamic of the new globalization. The scientific and technological advances generated under the wartime exigencies of the Second World War were eagerly adapted and put to use by the postwar civilian sector. In the 1960s and 1970s, for example, the introduction of fleets of large container-ships made possible the uninterrupted movement of goods in sealed cargo containers from their origin of manufacture to their ultimate destination across the ocean, stacked high on the ships' decks. Currently containerships can stack the containers twelve high on deck, carrying as many as a mind-boggling five thousand on a single voyage. Similarly, huge new wide-bodied aircraft began to take to the global skies, flying heavy cargo including the machinery of virtually an entire factory, to Bangkok, Bangladesh, or Beijing in less than a day, thus transporting production equipment or supplies at speeds and efficiencies hitherto undreamed of. This new aircraft capacity could, if desired, enable companies to make good on threats to move a plant elsewhere if conditions warranted.

Likewise, supertankers so large they need almost two miles to execute a turn at sea began to ply the oceans with a capacity many times that of earlier oil tankers, and with commensurately greater dangers to the natural environment in the event of an oil spill. Such advances in transportation capacity and volume have resulted in economies of scale that clearly tend to benefit those businesses and corporations able to support their cost.

The invention of the silicon chip in 1959 was the biggest single scientific discovery that set the world on the road to the new globalization. Spectacular progress in communications capabilities through fiber optics and satellites in outer space, and the quantum leap forward of information storage and retrieval that the steady development of computers began to achieve, transformed business and industrial capacity to network, share, and analyze information. Businesses, governments, and institutions at virtually all levels as well as millions of private citizens, both at home and abroad, began to avail themselves of these new capabilities. The result was that businesses and governments able to capitalize on these new capacities in major ways began to attain disproportionate power and influence.

In looking at these advances as they relate to the new globalism, Amartya Sen, a 1998 Nobel Laureate in economic science and a development economist, points to extensive evidence that the new global economy has brought prosperity to many different areas. But he adds that the main goal here is "how to make good use of the remarkable benefits of economic intercourse and technological progress in a way that pays adequate attention to the interests of the deprived and the underdog."[6] He notes that the principal challenge relates to inequality, and points to disparities in affluence and to "gross asymmetries in political, social, and economic opportunities and power." Sen also issues an important caveat against what he calls a Western chauvinist tendency to see globalization as the continuation of the great achievements of the West, now spreading to the world. He reminds us that going back many centuries, the active agents of globalization have been located far from the West, in China, India, and Arabia, whose mathematical, scientific, and technological discoveries were appropriated and built upon by the West over the centuries. In a similar vein, Richard Parker says we would all be more honest if we talked about our present era as part of a five-hundred-year-long chapter involving global Europeanization, not globalization. "We need to see how the legacy of specific changes in European-born political, economic, and value structures — not some 'natural' process — continues to define the current global era," says Parker.[7]

A Global Landscape Transformed

So much for two of the central dynamics propelling forward the new global economic engine: the new mobility and versatility of money, and the technological leaps in communications and transportation. What does a glance at the economic landscape of the globe over the last few decades reveal? It will be no surprise to find that the dominance and size of transnational corporations (TNCs) continue to be huge and growing. A recent study, treating giant global corporations together with countries as if they were "economies," found that of the world's hundred largest "economies," fifty-one are global corporations. Moreover, during the last generation, the world's five hundred largest TNCs have grown sevenfold in sales. Yet the top two hundred global corporations employed a total of only 18.8 million people. And corresponding to this growth in corporate wealth is the growth in the compensation packages of corporate executive officers. In 2002 the average compensation package of American CEOs was $10.83 million, growing 6 percent over the previous year in spite of enormous losses in the stock market. In 2001, executive pay was 411 times that of the average hourly worker. In 1980 this gap between worker and executive was only 42 to 1, according to the AFL-CIO's "executive pay watch" tabulations.

In the global financial industry it's natural to think first of the great international banks as centers of wealth: Chase Manhattan, Citicorp, and Bank of America, for example. Overseas banks such as the Bank of Tokyo, Sumitomo Bank, Deutsche Bank, or Barclays Bank are familiar names on the financial pages. As with the large transnational corporations, the story also is of the enlargement and concentration of financial assets. But here is a surprise: in the global financial landscape, these and other world banking powerhouses began to yield ground in the early 1980s to the emergence of international financial services companies when the big banks faced a debt repayment crisis by Third World countries that had begun to default on their loan payments. The British weekly magazine *The Economist* characterized this development as a huge shift in the international financial system over the past two decades.[8] Such financial services firms now engage in investment banking activities such as underwriting bond and equity issues, advising on mergers and acquisitions, and selling on loans to other investors — a broad diversification of activities and assets. Using international markets as their institutional focus, they reap extremely high levels of profitability. The complexity of such activities, and their relationship to actually promoting the economic well-being of peoples and nations in distant lands, is very difficult to assess. This complexity has far outstripped the ability of government regulatory agencies to understand and regulate their transactions. It is a shell game to end all shell games.

A third noteworthy aspect of the change in the global landscape is the emergence of the "global city" in the late twentieth century. There have been "global cities" for many centuries, of course. But the transformations in the world economy in the last two decades, and an accompanying shift toward a service economy, coupled with the fast-rising prominence and skyrocketing profitability of the new sector of international finance, have contributed to the rise of a new

kind of global city. The global cities of the new millennium do not
get our attention primarily because of their staggering populations —
although that definitely is an attention-getter. (According to United
Nations estimates for the year 2015, Mexico City will top the list at
27 million people. None of the top five cities in population will be in
Europe or the United States.) The new global cities are key because
they are the places where such accumulation of capital occurs and
from which the distribution of commodities and ideas is organized;
thus they have become the command-and-control centers of global
capitalism.[9]

In the new global city, the workforce required to keep the globalization engine moving forward obviously includes the financial, legal,
accounting, and analytical people one associates with modern-day
global business, plus the technological links: sophisticated communications technology, fiber-optic cables, air and rail transportation,
etc. But there is another crucial human component required for the
global city to operate, one inevitably overlooked: the huge and varied
service sector of low-wage workers. It is made up largely of immigrants to the city, migrating from overseas or from within the country,
with women predominating. These service workers are seldom recognized in global studies as part of the essential infrastructure required
to operate the global system, says sociologist Saskia Sassen.[10] They
are increasingly marginalized, both in their cramped living spaces in
the city, and in the ever-widening social and economic "distance"
between them and the people with whom many of them work in
close physical proximity, both in the gleaming skyscrapers and modern thoroughfares of the world's megacities, and also as domestic
workers in the homes of their corporate bosses. And not only corporate bosses: those of us who are middle class, who live in American
cities with a high immigrant population, gain hugely from the wage
disparity as we are serviced in our homes by maids, gardeners, and
babysitters.

Moreover, Sassen reminds us, the way up the economic ladder
for such workers — a ladder industrial workers of the mid-twentieth
century had succeeded in climbing — is blocked in this new labor

configuration. Large cities are thus seeing a demographic transformation: women, immigrants, and people of color, along with a declining middle class, relegated in servitude to the new elite.

Of central importance to all of these new developments in the global economy is the increasing prominence of international trade, epitomized by the three main financial and trade institutions that attempt to regulate global trade: the International Monetary Fund, the World Bank, and the World Trade Organization. They were created by the leading world economic powers, the IMF and the World Bank dating their history since the 1940s, the WTO being created in 1995. In chapter 8 I noted the IMF's oppressive lending practices to developing nations with regard to the debt repayment crisis facing these nations. These three groups are increasingly a focal point of widespread public debate. The world trade issues are very complex, but two stand out: the extent to which the liberalization of world trade, promoted through these three institutions, will address the endemic poverty and powerlessness in the poorest developing nations and here at home; and the extent to which the international trade rules agreed upon by nations participating in the World Trade Organization should take precedence over national governmental laws and policies. The policies of these three entities and their future direction are of vital importance to the attainment of a just global economic order.

Looking back at aspects of the global landscape just described, I've mentioned four landmarks, each of them in dynamic flux, and each interacting with the others:

- transnational corporations

- international banks and the rise of new financial institutions

- the new global city

- the key roles of the international financial and trade organizations

To these we can add a fifth aspect, one permeating the entire global order from top to bottom, yet one with the least audible voice and power, namely, those wage earners and would-be wage earners the world over.

These five component parts of the new global order are combining to push, pressure, and otherwise impact that political institution dominant in the world for at least two centuries, the nation-state. Intricately intertwined with these influences, each nation struggles to maintain its own agenda, which at its most bare-bones level means political survival for the party in power, economic prosperity (or its appearance), and the maintenance of at least a semblance of democratic order.

The Changing Political Landscape

I want here to highlight the political perspective in the United States that has formed the background for the huge changes I've just noted, namely, the sharply changing political landscape in our country over the last two decades (I would add here that political developments in the United Kingdom over the same period, and to a lesser extent the European continent, have followed the same general trend, with the same underlying political forces at work). The Merrill Lynch 1998 ad at the head of this chapter is a striking illustration of the newly articulated free-market ideology coming to the fore during that time. Pause for a moment to reflect on the breathtaking assertion in the title: "The World Is Ten Years Old." This ten-year-old world, born with the collapse of communism (marked by the 1989 fall of the Berlin Wall) is now said to be free for the first time in history to embrace "the emotions of the people," these seeming to be directly related to "the spread of free markets and democracy around the world." The world had no history before 1989, it implies. Even allowing for the hype widespread in the ad business, this ad could qualify as a quasi-religious statement — one comparable, say, to the second coming of Christ, but with salvation available in this world instead of the next, since people can now "turn their aspirations into achievements."

The appearance of this ad was not an aberration. It and assertions like it had their roots in the renaissance of a right-wing free-market ideology surfacing in the early 1980s with the founding of conservative think tanks such as the American Enterprise Institute and others. Francis Fukuyama's book *The End of History*, published in 1992, attracted great attention as it announced that the fall of communism had ended the competition between capitalism and communism, capitalism emerging triumphant, with no historical challenges to its dominance on the horizon. Another book, *The Commanding Heights*, written in 1998 by Daniel Yergin and Joseph Stanislaw, similarly staked the claim of capitalism's ultimate triumph. Its book jacket blurb was exultant in victory: "Trillions of dollars in assets and fundamental political power are changing hands as free markets wrest control from government of 'the commanding heights,' the dominant businesses and industries of the world economy." Note that in both the Merrill Lynch ad and *The Commanding Heights* the enemy is perceived to be government. *New York Times* columnist Thomas Friedman is similarly convinced that with the collapse of socialism, the way ahead for free-market capitalism is unimpeded.

So here is a twenty-first-century view of the Global Household, grounded in the belief that the unrestrained free market, through offering both maximum freedom of choice and the opportunity to succeed, will ultimately result in the well-being of more people than other economic systems or arrangements can provide. Its unifying principle is a new global capitalism, marvelously integrated through technology and communications, and proclaimed as the irresistibly rational economic ideology for the foreseeable future.

In this view the global economy is not *oikonomia* but a gated community. It excludes a world glimpsed with longing and aspiration by the workers at the Windows on the World restaurant atop the World Trade Center, and it excludes the liberating good news to the poor proclaimed by Jesus in his inaugural sermon at Nazareth. The beggar Lazarus remains outside the gate while the mansionization of wealth proceeds apace.

The good news is that despite the fanfare, this millennialist view of a new and unfettered capitalist ideology is coming under mounting criticism. In addition to the continuing worldwide protests against the new global capitalism, we have recently seen national governments begin to raise questions about the decisions and direction of the international trade organizations, most prominently the World Trade Organization. In September 2003 the discord reached unexpected heights with the collapse of the world trade talks sponsored by the WTO in Cancún, Mexico, primarily over the issue of agricultural policy toward developing nations. In what was widely regarded as a huge setback for the WTO, twenty-one developing nations succeeded in banding together to prevent plans being promoted by the United States and the European Union.

Also, the pervasive corporate scandals of Enron, WorldCom, Global Crossing, and others, while not sparking a widespread public backlash, have nonetheless had a dampening effect on public enthusiasm for the corporate dominance of economic life. And pretensions to global domination by the United States through both military and diplomatic aggression in Iraq and elsewhere have likewise caused widespread negative reaction throughout the world. Taken together, these reactions have clearly begun to lessen the attraction of unfettered global free-market policies espoused with such enthusiasm only five and six years ago.

Oikonomia and the Christian Global Household

In contrast to the "gated compound" of global capitalism, Christians can look at the same world and embrace a different Global Household: one that gathers in and embraces all sorts and conditions of men and women from every corner of the world, every station of life, and in every sphere of human activity, including our political, cultural, and economic life. This notion of a Global Household is not only a metaphor apt for our New Millennium world, it is also one deeply congruent with our religious history and its foundation: the biblical vision of "a world made new." For us it goes under another name: the kingdom of God. And as Kenneth Leech reminds us, the kingdom of God is the heart of the Christian gospel, the central metaphor of salvation.[11] It is rooted squarely in the life and ministry of Jesus, who identifies himself with its arrival upon earth (Mark 1:15). So here we can bring together *oikonomia*, the art of managing the Household, and the vision of the kingdom, which hovers over it.

We can clearly and consistently discern this holistic vision of the churches from their evolving attitudes toward wealth and poverty as well as their theology. And although the churches' putting this vision into practice in human affairs is very far from being sustained in all periods, its resurgence in unexpected times and places in history is testimony to our faith that God has not been left without witness at any time.

Such a perspective enables us as Christians to subject all economic systems to moral scrutiny — not just capitalist, but also the various socialist systems past and present as well as any economic system, either a combination of the two, or something else that may emerge. We are thus free to take positions on any economic policies or decisions affecting the human community in whole or in part. Moreover, we are free to set forth an alternative economic vision of the Household. In this sense, I believe, going back to the root of the word "economy" is a useful exercise. It helps us to understand that the economic system is the servant, not the master, of the Household, and that the moral and religious visions of a truly Global Household are inseparably linked.

This vision begins to take shape in the church of the first century, in the Acts of the Apostles and in several of the epistles. With Jesus' own words and actions as their foundation, the early Christians proceeded to apply them to the new community. As Julio de Santa Ana points out, the sense of unity that the Christians of Acts felt at the spiritual level had to be expressed at the material level as a sign of brotherly/sisterly community.[12] This primitive perspective on communal sharing and the condemnation of wealth are also mirrored in other early Christian writers outside the New Testament. Moreover, there is clear evidence that at least the first generation of Christians was heavily composed of those of low social condition — an indication of its communitarian appeal. Inevitably this began to change as Christianity grew rapidly and began to attract the more wealthy. By the second century, charity was no longer directed so clearly toward the eradication of poverty, but was directed toward opening people's minds to the implications of the spirit of love, observes de Santa Ana. With the conversion of the Emperor Constantine early in the fourth century, Christianity became the official religion of the empire; the radical communitarian ethic of the early church was submerged, largely moving into the monastic movement. So the *oikonomia* becomes the Empire — for good and for ill.

The medieval period saw the emergence of the Catholic Church in Europe into its dominant position in the West. The unitary vision of its mission expressed by the great medieval theologians came into prominence and held sway in the Christian world from the twelfth to the sixteenth century. Medieval society was viewed as a single social organism, says R. H. Tawney, the eminent British historian whose classic work *Religion and the Rise of Capitalism* (1926) has strongly influenced two generations of clergy and bishops in both England and America. The symbol of that social unity was the human body, wherein (following St. Paul) each member of society was held together by a system of mutual though varying obligations for the upbuilding of the whole. "The rigid medieval class structure notwithstanding, the fundamental assumptions of the medieval theologians were that economic interests are subordinate to the real business of life, which is salvation, and that economic conduct is an aspect of personal conduct, upon which ... the rules of morality are binding," writes Tawney. *"There is no place in medieval theory for economic activity which is not related to a moral end."*[13] As previously noted, an interesting footnote to the medieval period in which economic activity was subsumed under wider moral rules is that early in this period, a bellwether of the dangers that increased economic activity would in the future pose to the social fabric was glimpsed when avarice began to compete with pride at the top of the list of the Seven Deadly Sins.[14]

The medieval unitary vision came to an end in the sixteenth century with the fragmentation of the church in the Protestant Reformation, the sharply expanded economic activity of mercantile Europe, and the rise of capitalism. That vision remained largely submerged until the nineteenth century, when it began to reappear in England in mid-century, most prominently with F. D. Maurice, an Anglican clergyman. His influential work, *The Kingdom of Christ*, proclaimed the coming of Christ to be transformative not just for believers but for the entire human race. Maurice asserted that in the Incarnation of the Son of God, the whole realm of visible and invisible worlds had mystically been brought into close and inseparable union. Therefore everything that affects the world, i.e., every human activity, must become important to the Christian.[15]

Maurice's view of our Global Household — the *oikonomia* — and the right of the church to address it was also reaffirmed in the Roman Catholic Church, which reasserted its medieval social vision in two papal encyclicals amid worsening conditions for working people at the end of the nineteenth century, and again following the worldwide economic depression of the 1930s. Likewise, the social gospel movement in America early in the last century rediscovered the gospel in its fullness.[16]

Now, a century later, in response to the challenge posed by the new global capitalism, the churches are beginning to assert once again a more comprehensive global and theological vision of mission and ministry. The vision appears to be coming piecemeal, dribs and drabs here and there, with some theological and social analysis just beginning to find its way into book-length treatment. One very helpful if short treatise within the Anglican Communion is by Laurie Green, a bishop in the Church of England. Green reaffirms a theology of the Incarnation as the ground upon which to formulate a new urban theology that is adequate to address twenty-first-century globalization. "It would seem [in St. John's Gospel] that Jesus is not simply showing us that in our Christian community the local is in the universal and the universal in the local, but that both are inclusive of the other, for all are held in unity by something much deeper — namely, the indwelling presence of the creator God," he writes.[17]

So the intellectual task of the Christian churches in our time is enormous, and is twofold. First, we must apply ourselves to become knowledgeable about both the critical components and workings of this global capitalism of the twenty-first century, and its underlying economic and social assumptions. Second, we must embark upon the historical and theological task of "reclaiming lost ground" — the lost and neglected ground of our very own history and theology, one firmly rooted in the Bible. The recovery of this past social tradition in its fullness, and its record of engagement with contemporary social and economic conditions, will form the base for our active, programmatic response today.

The great vulnerability of the new global capitalism is its total lack of any moral vision for humankind — a lack compounded by increasing evidence that this system is carrying the world community toward unprecedented crisis. In sharp contrast, a Christian moral vision proclaiming release for the captives and good news to the poor has the power to free up both the poor and the rich for the possibility of a new world of justice, peace, and human brotherhood and sisterhood. The great challenge facing not only the Christian churches, but the interfaith community in partnership with them, is to formulate goals and strategies for effective engagement with the issues of globalization. To do this involves beginning to sort out critical public policy choices at the global level, and also at national and regional levels.

For Reflection and Discussion

1. When you read in the newspapers the latest news about the economy, to what extent do you think it is a balanced presentation? What is missing, or what is underemphasized?

2. In the section on "A Global Landscape Transformed," which of the five aspects mentioned concerns you most, and why? In the new global city described by Saskia Sassen, do you encounter any of the workers in the service sector? If so, where?

3. Can the churches begin to relate the Global Household (*oikonomia*) to the kingdom of God in Christian education programs for both adults and children? If so, how?

Chapter Eleven

Public Policy Choices in the New Global Economic Order

The increasingly vehement worldwide reaction against the policies that drive globalization is a significant change. . . . It is the trade unionists, students, environmentalists — ordinary citizens — marching in the streets of Prague, Seattle, Washington, and Genoa who have put the need for reform on the agenda of the developed world.

—Joseph E. Stiglitz, former chief economist, The World Bank[1]

We cannot allow those who wield economic power to govern on one criterion of economic profitability. . . . We have to take responsibility for our world, for our economic system, harnessing it to serve us, rather than allowing it to enslave us.

—Njongonkulu Ndungane, archbishop of Capetown, South Africa, address to the Los Angeles World Affairs Council, June 2000

Let justice roll down like waters,
and righteousness like an ever-flowing stream.

—Amos 5:24

H ERE ARE THREE recent stories that dramatize the urgent need to adopt new public policies in the era of the new global capitalism: The first is from a television documentary focusing on workers in Thailand. The workers, who work at the Bed and Bath Prestige factory in Bangkok, report for their early morning shift. To their surprise they find the factory's gates padlocked. Incredulous at first — one of the workers tells the interviewer that her first thought was, "They've got to let us in, there's an important shipment that has to go out today" — they realize with a jolt that their jobs have evaporated overnight: gone. Wages owed them were not paid; no severance pay was given, even though these were requirements under Thailand's

147

labor laws. The company, which made clothing for Reebok, Nike, and Levi Strauss, had simply locked the doors and left.

In a show of defiance rare in Thailand, the 350 affected workers, being unable to directly protest a management that had abandoned its own factory, decided to occupy the courtyard of the Ministry of Labor in Bangkok. They set up a "live-in," camping there until the government responded. Head-to-head talks began with ministry officials. "Just follow what is written in the [Thai] Constitution; we ask no more than that," the protest leader told them, but no progress was reported. A ministry spokesperson explained that the government "had to balance between worker's interests and investor's interests," and that if workers' actions are going to chase away investors, that cannot be tolerated. For three months, drawing widespread press coverage, the workers stayed encamped at the Labor Ministry compound, even as their numbers dwindled to 150. Finally the government decided to give the remaining protesters (not the 200 who had left) a cash settlement of $448 each. In Thailand this was considered a victory for the workers.[2]

The second story involves small farmers in the Philippines, whose government had enthusiastically joined the World Trade Organization at its inception in 1995. Embracing the free-market gospel, the farmers would now have access to global markets for their farm products, went the reasoning, their cheap labor being their chief asset. The Philippine government predicted that this new access would create half a million farm jobs a year, improving also the country's trade balance. But they failed to grasp the harsh realities of the world trade game. The harshest of these realities was, and is, the huge subsidies that the U.S. government and the European Union pay to their own farmers (who are frequently large agricultural conglomerates), thus making their products artificially cheap on the world market. In the case of the United States, farmers receive as much as $3 billion annually in subsidies. In no way can a peasant farmer in a poor country compete under these conditions. On the island of Mindanao after the WTO agreement, farmers growing corn saw their prices fall so steeply that it was not worth harvesting and was left in the field. "Put simply, the Philippines got taken," editorialized the *New York Times* on this subject. Since joining the WTO the Philippines has lost hundreds of thousands of farming jobs.[3]

The third story involves the dream of Roberto Chávez, a Mexican immigrant to the United States, and thousands like him over the years. He came to the United States in the mid-1980s as a twenty-year-old from the state of Chihuahua and eventually found a good job, enabling him to buy a home and raise his five children. His wife also found a job as an assembly worker. In 1995 the North American Free Trade Agreement (NAFTA) was enacted into law amid great fanfare. But in 1998 Roberto lost his job of fifteen years as a warehouseman. His company closed its doors and moved to Mexicali, just across the Mexican border, where workers were paid much lower wages — ten to fifteen dollars a day to start. Within months, Roberto's wife also lost her job. Writes reporter Evelyn Iritani: "Today, the more likely victims of what Ross Perot called a 'giant sucking sound' are the [U.S.] Latino workers in textiles, food processing and electronics, many of whom risked their lives to cross the border, only to see their new jobs go south as companies sought cheap labor."[4]

Such stories serve as a window through which to glimpse the stark social contrasts that have increasingly come to typify the evolution of the new global economic order. On the one hand are the aspirations and demands of the world's poorest families, who work hard, play by the rules, and struggle to survive on low wages in oppressive working conditions. On the other are the blinkered decisions of corporations, governments, and international trade organizations whose mind-sets are locked into rigid economic ideologies, rules that seemingly take small account of the human and social impact of those decisions.

The Public Policy Challenge: Structural and Attitudinal

We know that in the new globalization of the last few decades the world has slid deeper into global poverty at the same time it is seeing increased wealth concentrating at the top. This reality is overwhelmingly the principal challenge to public policy across the board, from global to local levels. But our primary challenge is at bottom not just one of advocating new economic policies to address these inequities. It is the more serious task of breaking free from the shackles of an economic determinism that in our time has elevated itself to dogma in the "free market" approach to the world economic order; and to look at the world once more as one indissolubly human community bound together: "One World, Ready or Not," as the title of William Greider's book has it. If nations can put aside theory and confront what is occurring; if they have the courage to impose remedial changes before it is too late, we can avoid disaster, says Greider. Similarly, Joseph Stiglitz, speaking as an insider (both at the IMF and the World Bank) urgently calls the bureaucrats there to put aside their ideological mind-sets and approach problems with a new openness.

From a Christian perspective, we have not only our own rich traditions to draw upon, but also new religious approaches to globalization. As the millennium year 2000 approached, the Christian churches around the globe, and others also, embraced the biblical concept of Jubilee, based upon the divine exhortation in the book of Leviticus (chapter 25) to "proclaim liberty throughout the land," and launched the Jubilee 2000 Campaign.[5] Out of this campaign many church curricula were developed for the purpose of promoting church participation. Typically they embraced a global perspective. One national curriculum highlighted four basic needs of the global human family: to nurture, protect, and celebrate God's creation; to share the wealth of the world equitably and with a true sense of justice; to release human beings from all forms of captivity (such as the physical slavery still existing today in many forms); and to restore community through reconciliation and respect.

Likewise seizing upon the new millennium as opportunity, in September 2000 the United Nations, in a formal vote, adopted its own vision of a renewed world community, calling it the Millennium

Declaration. The eight goals of this declaration committed the international community to an expanded vision of development, one that "vigorously promotes human development as the key to sustaining social and economic progress in all countries, and recognizes the importance of creating a global partnership for development." Setting the year 2015 as the date for achieving such goals, the declaration also set specific targets for each goal so as to be able to measure progress. The eight goals address extreme poverty and hunger, universal primary education, equality and empowerment for women, reduction of child mortality, improvement of maternal health, combating HIV/AIDS, ensuring environmental sustainability, and the development of a partnership for global development. So we have these two formulations — one theological, the other programmatic — as a guiding moral backdrop for public policy considerations.

For purposes of our discussion, when we say "public policy" we mean the laws, regulations, or agreements formal or informal, entered into by international bodies (the United Nations, the IMF, the World Bank, the WTO, NAFTA, and others) and nations; and also the economic development policies of states or municipalities that have to do directly or indirectly with the global economic order. In the case of states or cities, such policies may be less obviously related to the global economy, but it is very important to understand that there can be a global causal relationship at lower levels, especially when considering action strategies.

The global imperative for advocating alternative public policies should by now be quite clear. It arises from the urgent need to "impose some order on the global marketplace, to make both finance and commerce more accountable for the consequences of their actions, and to give hostage societies more ability to determine their own future," in William Greider's words.[6] Against this backdrop, broad policy recommendations can emerge for church consideration. The recommendations that follow are a broad sample of what is currently under discussion by a wide segment of opinion as alternatives to the present global economic order.

Public Policies for the
International and National Arenas

◆ Reform the international rules of trade

◆ Maintain national sovereignty over corporate profits

◆ Advocate food sovereignty, especially for developing nations

◆ Impose international restrictions on the global movement of capital

◆ Cancel Third World debt

◆ End the legal fiction of corporations as persons

◆ Strengthen international labor standards and build strong unions

◆ Make environmental sustainability an ironclad requirement for development projects

◆ Ensure the upholding of human rights as defined by the United Nations Universal Declaration of Human Rights

Reform the international rules of trade. In what could be a watershed year, 2003 saw broad and mounting resistance to the unfettered free-trade approach. This resistance is now at many levels: from the streets, to newly coordinated strategies among the developing nations, to conferences and pronouncements of prominent development economists and Nobel Prize winners, to the editorials of prominent newspapers, and to the halls and tribunals of the trade bodies themselves. The international trade policies promoted by the WTO, the IMF, and the World Bank that have pressured developing nations to open themselves to free trade, privatize public investments, and reduce government controls as conditions for financial assistance seem destined for significant modification or even outright elimination. Moreover, proposed regional trade agreements such as the Free Trade Area of the Americas (FTAA) are running into heavy seas as they try to chart a course forward. In October 2003 the thirty-eight-nation FTAA meeting in Miami, encountering significant protests inside and outside the conference, was forced to conclude that its target date of signing an agreement by the end of 2004 would not be met.

Another free trade proposal, the Central American Free Trade Agreement (CAFTA), has also recently been criticized for its failure to affect "the lives and dignity of poor families and vulnerable workers whose voice should receive special attention," according to a joint statement issued by Central American and U.S. Catholic bishops. The July 2004 statement followed the signing of the trade agreement between the United States and five Central American nations. The bishops' concern included the impact of the treaty's provisions upon Central American farmers, the need for clearer enforcement mechanisms for the protection of worker rights, and the protection of the environment. "Human solidarity must accompany economic integration so as to preserve community life, protect families and livelihoods, and defend local cultures," said the bishops. Despite widespread opposition from many Third World nations the agreement passed in the U.S. Senate by a close vote in July 2005. It was also approved by the House of Representatives after intense White House lobbying.

A chief complaint of poor nations is that existing trade agreements have been concocted almost totally out of public view by economic and business elites in the developed nations, and that real participation by the developing nations in the decision-making process has been virtually nonexistent. At the September 2003 World Trade Organization meeting in Cancún, for example, a coalition of grassroots organizations from Thailand, routinely excluded like others from the organization's deliberations, dramatized their exclusion by issuing an open letter to the U.S. government and the European Union. In it, voices from that Asian country representing peasants' networks, slum dwellers, a laborer's network, and an alternative agriculture network called on the WTO for specific reforms. Among these were a call to cease negotiations toward a new round of trade liberalization; undertake a thorough review of both the implementation and the environmental and social impact of existing trade rules and agreements in relation to medicine, food, fisheries, and agriculture; and initiate measures to remove food and agriculture from the control of the WTO. Their demands found resonance when twenty-one developing nations walked out in protest of U.S. and European governments' refusal to significantly reduce agricultural subsidies to their farmers, causing the collapse of the agricultural trade talks. Chastened by this defeat, the wealthy nations of the WTO reached an accord with developing nations in July 2004, to work to eventually eliminate the huge farm subsidies they have enjoyed. Notwithstanding, some developing nations continued to be skeptical that real change would be seen for its farmers.

The poignant letter by the Thai grassroots group would also resonate deeply with the 350 locked-out workers at Bangkok's Bed and Bath factory, and with the Filipino farmers of Mindanao whose corn crop was left in the field. It highlights a public policy imperative: "No globalization without representation!"

In this regard Joseph Stiglitz — indisputably an "establishment" figure — notes that current voting membership in the IMF board consists chiefly of finance ministers and central bank governors from the developed countries. Representation from the supposed recipients of IMF aid is almost totally lacking — not to mention ordinary farmers and workers. A similar situation exists at the other international financial and trade bodies; the notion of any participatory democracy in their deliberations seems never to have occurred to them. The crucial task, says Stiglitz, is to work toward change in the governance and voting rights of these bodies in order that voices from the developing nations can have real weight. Even the churches — as slow as we are to heed the implications of our own religious beliefs — learned back in the 1960s in our community work to include people affected in decisions affecting their lives.

In trade disputes, national sovereignty must trump corporate profits. The need for national laws to remain paramount in the face of the drive for profits by multinational corporations was a crucial topic discussed at a Conference on Humanizing the Global Economy, sponsored by the Canadian, U.S., and Latin American Conferences of Catholic Bishops in January 2002 in Washington. In a paper prepared for the conference by a social commission of the Canadian bishops, the authors of this commission addressed a particularly reprehensible aspect of the North American Free Trade Agreement (NAFTA), called the Investor-State Mechanism in the trade jargon, and sometimes referred to as "chapter 11." Under this mechanism corporations won a newfound power: to sue states (countries) for perceived loss of profit due to governmental "restrictions" on their activities (yes, you read that sentence correctly!). The commission report to the Canadian bishops, using a case study of an ongoing dispute, noted that the chapter 11 provision raises profound issues for state sovereignty and its capacity — for example, to legally provide environmental protection to its citizens, and by implication uphold the democratic participation of people in their own governance.

The case study at the Washington conference involved a dispute between Methanex, a Canadian multinational corporation, and the United States, being considered under the litigation procedures of NAFTA. The dispute arose in 1999 after the State of California ordered the phasing out of the chemical MTBE, a methanol-based additive to gasoline California had been purchasing in large quantities from the Methanex Corporation. The decision to phase out arose from concerns that leakage of the additive from underground gasoline storage tanks would begin to contaminate California's groundwater. But under the new NAFTA rule it is permissible for corporations to claim damages. That is exactly what Methanex did, suing the U.S. government for $970 million, and claiming before the NAFTA adjudication tribunal that among other losses, its share price and potential revenues have been drastically affected by the controversy, amounting (astounding as the logic may seem) to an expropriation of its future profits due to lower sales. Even the American government, at least in this case, is contesting the corporation's claim to preempt federal environmental laws as a usurpation of national sovereignty. Yet such are the complexities in which NAFTA has enveloped itself that, incredibly, this major case is still not completely adjudicated. The NAFTA tribunal heard the case in June 2004; a final decision was still pending as of mid-2005. The right to corporate profits vs. national sovereignty: even national governments have begun to raise questions about the ramifications of their own free-trade policies.

And not only national sovereignty may be threatened under the regulations governing international trade agreements. Proposed service and procurement rules under both the WTO and the proposed Free Trade Area of the Americas agreement could undermine state or municipal living wage laws, prevailing wage laws, and service contract laws on the theory that their effect could be seen as "impacting the conditions of competition" — i.e., impairing "pro-market" mechanisms that lie at the heart of the new globalization — in ways that might "disadvantage" foreign companies providing services to the United States.

From these examples we can see that fundamental changes in international trade policy and decision-making processes are imperative. Some groups, such as the International Forum on Globalization, a group of prominent economists and other academics from both the developed and the developing world, are going so far as to call for the "decommissioning," or abolition, of the WTO, the IMF, and the World Bank, and the marked strengthening of the United Nations and its leading agencies such as the UN Conference on Trade and Development (UNCTAD) or the Economic and Social Council. The International Forum notes that the latter body was intended at the creation of the UN to assume responsibility for global and economic affairs.[7] Short of such a "decommissioning" of these bodies, we should support calls for a major reordering of trade priorities toward respecting the rights and needs of the peoples of developing countries, and in particular to require the IMF and other trade groups to place highest priority on the specific local and regional labor and environmental impacts of a pending trade agreement.

Advocate food sovereignty. Food sovereignty, as defined by Via Campesina (the world's largest farmers organization, which includes landless workers and women farmers) is "the human right of all peoples and nations to grow food in ways that are culturally, ecologically and economically appropriate for them." Anuradha Mittal, codirector of Food First and the Institute for Food and Development Policy, maintains that food sovereignty is the fundamental issue at stake in ongoing WTO agricultural agreement negotiations. The current rules operate to keep power squarely in the hands of export producers, large businesses, and elites, at the expense of family farmers, says Mittal.[8] Advocating such a policy is in fact a continuation in a more systemic way of the long-standing goals of many churches in addressing world hunger.

Impose international restrictions on the global movement of capital. In the last chapter we saw the uses to which Barbara Garson's $29,500 investment was put as she tracked its movements around the world. There was no necessary correlation between the uses to which her money was put and the creation of jobs or wealth for those needing them. Both internationally and nationally, new laws and regulations are necessary to begin to require banks to use their funds more to strengthen job-creating enterprises and less to create wealth for their investors. One example of the excessive movements of capital receiving more public attention recently (even by some in Congress) is the role of major offshore banking centers such as those in Bermuda, the Cayman Islands, and other places. Offshore banking practices legitimize the scandalous arrangements that permit investors to hide their money from the banking and security laws of their own governments, egregiously evading the payment of income taxes. International law should outlaw the existence of these offshore centers. Reform advocates say that if only a few governments in the wealthy nations could be persuaded to prohibit their own banking systems — in the case of the United States this would be the Federal Reserve Bank — from honoring the transfers of offshore capital, these tax havens might become history.

Another recent example of efforts to turn public policy more toward the regulation of money transactions in order to assist in real economic development is the Tobin Tax Initiative. This initiative, gaining in support over the years since Canada voted in 1999 to support it in principle, spotlights the massive amounts of currency trades occurring on the international financial markets (more than $1.8 trillion daily). In this daily mind-boggling exchange of money across the globe, the currency market has become a kind of global casino.

Watching their global "green screens," investors bet huge sums of currency daily on whether, for example, the Mexican peso or the Thai baht will rise or fall in value over against the dollar or other strong currency, and frequently realize colossal profits. The Tobin initiative, supported by key groups such as the World Council of Churches, the AFL-CIO, Global Exchange, and several others, would tax currency sales at 0.1 to 0.25 percent of a given transaction. The tax would discourage lucrative short-term speculative trades but leave long-term productive investments intact. The revenue from the Tobin tax initiative would amount to $100 billion–$300 billion a year, according to its advocates. Such a substantial pot of money, properly and democratically administered by an appropriate international body, could be used for the urgent development needs of the poorer nations.

Cancel Third World debt. A previous chapter traced the origins of the financial indebtedness owed by Third World nations, and the huge long-term burden placed on them to repay these debts;[9] loan repayments for some nations have constituted as much as 40 percent of their annual income. The success of the Jubilee 2000 campaign in marshaling the support of the international religious community to pressure the developed countries to cancel more than $1.3 billion annually of the debt owed by the twenty-six Heavily Indebted Poor Countries (HIPCs) needs to continue unrelenting, for this amount represents only a third of the total indebtedness owed by the poor nations to the wealthy nations. The churches should continue to press the United States and the wealthy nations for total debt cancellation.

In the last two decades, an international tragedy compounding the deep indebtedness of the poorest nations has been unfolding in Africa, and also in Asia: the AIDS pandemic. There was considerable fanfare in the global community in January 2003 when President Bush announced his $15 billion global AIDS initiative. But the gift has turned out to be "tightly bound in red tape," according to an international coalition of nonprofit organizations. The red tape establishes a complex maze of conditions under which those nations desperate to obtain retroviral AIDS drugs in their countries may buy or import generic versions of the drugs. The big problem is the pharmaceutical industry lobby, which, fearing loss of its profit margins, is resisting plans to amend existing patent laws and allow the manufacture of cheaper generic drugs for wide distribution. Moreover, only a few months after the promise of $15 billion to fight AIDS over a five-year period, it became known that the first year's installment from the United States would be reduced to $2 billion or even less, from the initial planned $3 billion. So the push for total debt cancellation must recognize the staggering economic impact of the AIDS pandemic on the resources of African and Asian nations, and also include policy initiatives to meet the tragedy of the AIDS pandemic so that generic drugs become widely available in the acutely suffering countries of Africa and Asia.

End the legal fiction of a corporation as a person. Policies to reform the international rules of trade, and to restrict the movements of large amounts of capital across the globe would themselves begin to significantly address the need to limit the huge influence that large corporations have over global development. Likewise, wider compliance with international labor standards and the reform of labor law in the United States to more decisively protect working people's right to organize would curb corporate power. However, there are two areas of corporate reform that can be more specifically addressed. One involves the current law (established in 1886 by the U.S. Supreme Court) that establishes that a private corporation is a "person," and as such is entitled to the legal rights and protection the Constitution affords to any person. This equation of persons with property, says David Korten, establishes a presumed right of the corporation to the security of its property and its profit over a person's right to a means of living. In effect "that [1886] law connected political rights to property rather than to the person," says Korten, "an idea that to this day carries the seed of democracy's undoing."[10] In a British context, but one applicable to this issue a century and a half later, Charles Kingsley, a nineteenth-century Anglican social reformer, spoke fervently to the heart of the matter from a moral and religious perspective:

I entreat you, I adjure you, to trust the Bible, the true Radical Reformer's Guide...We have preached the rights of property and the duties of labor, when God knows, for every once that it does that, [the Bible] preaches ten times over the duties of property and the rights of labor.[11]

Although the 1886 Supreme Court decision has long since been accepted unquestioningly, we should find ways to work for legislative reform of the chartering, i.e., the incorporation, of large corporations by the state, so as to begin to differentiate between the rights of persons and the rights — and duties — of corporations. Such reforms might begin by requiring corporations to meet certain labor and environmental standards that are in the public interest before they are legally chartered. They might be required to pay living wages to their workers, and to agree to pay substantial penalties should they decide to transfer their workers offshore, as a condition of being granted a charter to do business.

Strengthen international labor standards and build strong unions. At the core of our insistence upon minimum standards for the working conditions of people lie two principles that find resonance in the Christian tradition: first, the inherent dignity of work as a human enterprise directed both toward personal creative fulfillment and the wider upbuilding of the human community; and second, the understanding of workers not as a commodity to be bought and sold, but as "human capital" — a precious asset at the heart of the productive process. The International Labor Organization, a member agency of the United Nations, is the long-established (since 1919) international benchmark institution for the maintenance and furtherance of international labor standards. It deserves to be much better known and supported in the United States. In its founding statement the ILO seeks among other things to "maintain the link between social progress and economic growth, and the guarantee of fundamental principles and rights at work." Foremost among the policies it upholds are: freedom of association in the workplace, i.e., the right to organize; the abolition of forced labor (for example, in the

large-scale importation of prostitutes into developing countries in recent years); the elimination of child labor; and the elimination of
discrimination (race, ethnic, gender) with respect to employment and
occupation. These and other policies are promoted through instruments called "conventions" of the ILO, to which member states sign
on, and "recommendations," which set out guidelines for national
labor rights policies or actions. The international reach and flexibility
of large corporations makes it very difficult to present a coordinated
and effective labor strategy that builds international solidarity among
workers. However, the ILO does serve as a very important and visible educational forum through its regional conferences, and also as
an administrative tribunal that can hear labor disputes.

One such complaint, lodged with the ILO in 2003 by some labor
unions in El Salvador, illustrates the complex — and complicit —
nature of the opposition to workers. The Salvadoran government
(significantly, not a signatory to the ILO conventions), in negotiations
with the International Monetary Fund and the World Bank for major
loan agreements, acceded to the "conditionalities" placed upon it
for loan approvals, namely, that the government privatize designated
agencies. In their complaint to the ILO, the unions charged that government workers were illegally dismissed, harassed by armed guards,
or offered reduction in employment status when they protested the
new requirements. This case clearly dramatizes the need to establish
polices and procedures that permit organized labor and community
groups to have an effective voice in such disputes, and is also a specific illustration of what is wrong with current international loan
requirements.

*Make environmental sustainability an ironclad requirement for
proposed development projects.* The global capitalist engine of the
twenty-first century is simply not compatible with the urgent need
to prevent its industrial and economic activities from destroying the
global ecological balance. The evidence for this assertion has risen
to a crescendo in the last three decades. The Report on Alternatives
to Economic Globalization puts it this way: "Economic globalization is intrinsically harmful to the environment because it is based

on ever-increasing consumption, exploitation of resources, and waste disposal problems."[12] The depletion of the Earth's ozone layer; rising temperatures and freakish weather patterns; rainforest destruction; the steady depletion of groundwater; the proliferation of nuclear wastes; the pending mass production of genetically altered foodstuffs, seed, and animals; and other environmental threats constitute dire testimony to a basic incompatibility existing between the present global economic dynamic and the global environment.

The clash between environmental sustainability and the relentless need for corporate capitalism to maintain and expand its markets is epitomized in the Methanex Corporation's dispute with the State of California. Water is also at issue in other even more dramatic ways, for example with India's multibillion-dollar Narmada Valley Dam project. In reality this project consists of not one, but over thirty large dams, and numerous small ones across India — all intended to harness the waters of the Narmada River and its tributaries for electrical power, and requiring the submergence of many square miles of arable land, plus the planned displacement and resettlement of 35 million people. Granted, there is an urgent and undeniable need for India to irrigate croplands to grow more food for its burgeoning population. But were there not other ways to achieve this goal that might have put India's ecosystem, and many millions of people, at less risk?

Environmental leaders, acutely conscious of the many "after the fact" environmental disasters — that is, disasters not anticipated at the time of a project's inception — have proposed an environmental policy concept known as "the Precautionary Principle." This principle, already adopted by Germany and Sweden, establishes that if a product or practice raises potentially significant threats to human health or the environment, action may be taken to restrict, delay, or prohibit its introduction. The proponents of the Principle assert that the burden of proof of the harmlessness of a new technology, process, activity, or chemical lies with the proponents, not with the general public. We should advocate the adoption of this Principle as an integral component of the policies and procedures of the World Trade

Organization and the various other international trade groups and associations, thus reversing the almost universal current practice both in and beyond the trade organizations of placing the burden upon community groups or governmental entities to prove environmental damage.

Uphold international human rights as defined by the United Nations Universal Declaration of Human Rights. The Declaration, subscribed to by member states of the UN, is the moral undergirding for the principal civil and political goals aspired to by all who strive for the creation of a just and peaceful global community. The Declaration includes such rights as "a standard of living adequate for... health and well-being, including food, clothing, housing, and medical care, and necessary social services, and the right to security in the event of unemployment..." In recent years, these rights have been interpreted to include the cultural rights of peoples to preserve their cultural and historical heritage in the face of economic and consumerist pressures.

Addressing Globalization at Local and State Policy Levels

Are the economic development policies and practices of our cities and states related to the larger currents of the new globalization? Absolutely. Global corporate and financial power in the twenty-first century is exactly that: global. The same corporations and banks that are consolidating their power and presence in Bangladesh, China, Mexico, and Argentina are also expanding their influence in our cities and states. They seek the same legislative advantages: tax breaks, reduction or suspension of labor and worker safety laws, the setting aside of environmental and social standards, and other lucrative benefits that have characterized their global operations. The resulting rise in low-wage poverty in the United States — now fully 20 percent of the workforce, or 26 million people earning $8.23/hr. or less — mirrors the global stagnation of wages and increased poverty in the last twenty years.

Over against these trends in our cities and states, however, surprisingly effective new movements and strategies have developed and are beginning to lead to new government policies to address this poverty imbalance. Chief among them is the living wage movement. To date the movement, active across the country in small and large cities and on college campuses, has achieved the passage of living wage ordinances in over 116 cities, with several dozens more pending. Moreover, the movement has gained a foothold in Britain; after many months of work, the living wage campaign in East London, waged by The East London Community Organization (TELCO), succeeded in January 2004 in persuading Barclays Bank to set "living wage" pay and other benefits including holidays and pension entitlements for cleaners and domestic workers under contract to it. This was a hard-won victory for TELCO, which brought churches, community groups, and unions together to "give a voice to the invisible and marginal workforce that keeps the City of London going," according to a BBC news program.

Why is the living wage movement a globalization issue? The reason may not be immediately obvious. It is a response at municipal levels to the increased poverty in our cities resulting from at least three trends, the first two of which are also prominent at global levels: expanded free-market opportunities flowing from lower taxation and regulation of business, the privatization of government services, and (in the case of the United States) the flood of immigrants from Mexico, Central America, and the Caribbean in recent years. The new immigration flows have proven a bonanza across the country for businesses seeking low-wage, nonunion labor. In many cities across the South, the local police are having to take rudimentary Spanish lessons in order to communicate with the new immigrant workforce materializing in large numbers to do the low-wage work in the food-processing, textile, and other industries there. And from Seattle to Omaha to the cities and towns of New England, the story is the same: workers and their families from the developing world, desperate to escape the increasing poverty of their native lands, come northward seeking to survive.

Living wage ordinances began to confront these neo-Dickensian realities of our twenty-first-century cities beginning in the mid-1990s by demanding that living wages be paid to workers whose employers have city contracts and receive public subsidies or tax breaks. The strongest ordinances also require health benefits plus paid vacation and sick days, and apply also to part-time employees. Although the ordinances affect a proportionately small number of workers within their communities, their existence is a boost to organized labor, setting a wage standard that becomes visible to the entire community. So by enacting such ordinances, municipal governments put business on notice that they have a social responsibility to the community to pay more than poverty wages, especially if they are receiving financial incentives and highly favored contracts. Moreover, the living wage movement calls attention to the gross inadequacy of the current federal minimum wage of $5.15 an hour — a scandalous one-third or less of what is currently needed to lift a family of four out of poverty.

Growing out of the living wage movement but going considerably further is a campaign in Los Angeles to require a Community Impact Report (CIR). This campaign, in full swing through a powerful coalition headed by the Los Angeles Alliance for a New Economy, is pushing for a municipal law that would require potential developers to meet minimum social and economic standards from the community's standpoint. A developer would have to ensure that a project would pay living wage jobs, hire from the surrounding neighborhood, meet specified affordable housing needs, provide certain neighborhood services, provide green space, and meet other requirements before the project receives the green light from the city. The Los Angeles campaign pushing for a municipal law to make a CIR a standard requirement for economic development projects is being closely watched by consumer and labor groups around the country. It should become a standard public policy requirement for cities everywhere. In fact, so as not to let the grass grow under anyone's feet, four California groups have joined recently to form a "California Partnership for Working Families" to work long-term toward elevating this public policy requirement to a statewide level. Thus, the expanding living wage movement and the expansion of worker and community rights and benefits at municipal and state levels are key public policy counterparts to global policy measures and strategies. These lower-level policy objectives become crucial and highly visible pressure points that help make the link with policies at the global international level.

So the policy choices suggested in this chapter and others that may be put forth can help us in two ways. One, they can help define what the political paths to a different and more just global economic order — an alternative to the present trajectory of globalization — might look like. Two, at whatever levels we in the religious community might work — local, regional, or national — they are a concrete reminder that our work must be done within a global perspective. They serve to help us remain in sync with the Big Picture. And they remind us that we have to be political, practical, and strategic in working to implement a religious vision of the Global Household — a.k.a., for Christians, the kingdom of God.

For Reflection and Discussion

1. Of the three examples at the beginning of this chapter dramatizing the need for new public policies, which is the most interesting to you, and why?

2. In this chapter, nine public policy choices are suggested as possibilities for addressing globalization. Which are the most interesting or compelling to you? Which of them do you think your church or community might most effectively address?

3. In thinking of your own city or town, see if you can identify economic issues affecting it that have their roots in corporate or governmental global practices.

Chapter Twelve

Making Connections
with the Global

The Churches in Action

*No social advance rolls in on the wheels of inevitability. It comes through the
tireless efforts of dedicated individuals.*

— Martin Luther King Jr.

*Struggle does not have to be hard; it has to be full of joy, for life is stronger
than death! Let us not waste our energy in anger, but on the joy of working
with the people.*

— Julia Esquivel, Guatemalan poet

Joshua fit the battle of Jericho, an' the walls came tumblin' down.

— Traditional Negro spiritual

SOMETIME IN THE 1990s — before the 1999 "Battle of Seattle" —
a new connectedness of people began to appear across the globe.
It was a connectedness different from the global electronic and board-
room "old-boy" connectedness of corporations and banks in pursuit
of profits, and different from that of governments and international
trade organizations. It was outside these spheres. This connectedness — a sign of great hope amid widespread cynicism and despair
over the direction of world events — includes, but isn't limited to,
nonprofit organizations, farmers' cooperatives, trade unions at the
local as well as national level, peasant and worker organizations,
peace groups, environmental groups, academic think tanks and special research projects, grassroots religious groups as well as world
religious leaders, and even some prominent Establishment figures
(George Soros, Joseph E. Stiglitz). The connectedness has a name:
global civil society.

This new phenomenon clearly signals a greater involvement of the world's citizens in shaping a common future, according to British social scientists who are studying the phenomenon.[1] Its existence goes against the conventional political discourse of a world seemingly dominated by nation-states and transnational corporations. This new global civil society represents "the sphere of ideas, values, organizations, networks, and individuals located primarily outside the institutional complexes of family, market, and state, and beyond the confines of national societies, polities, and economics.... Global Society is also about the meaning and practice of human equality in an increasingly unjust world."[2]

Notwithstanding the deep pessimism and fear for the future of the world five years into the new millennium, there can be little doubt of the significance of this new presence. The global antiwar protests of early 2003, putting as many as 11 million people from eight hundred cities around the world into the streets in a single day to protest the impending Iraq war, was a dramatic sign that there is a second "superpower" out there, capable of being awakened to question conventional power and militarism. As well, the annual World Social Forums, drawing as many as a hundred thousand people from all over the world to Porto Alegre, Brazil, in 2003, and an equal number to Bombay, India, in 2004, testify to this new level of interest, as well as the need for people to network and strategize. The phenomenon is viewed as a mediating third domain between the intensive privatization efforts of global capitalism, and the policies of national governments that are most often hand-in-glove with that of corporate and financial power.

It is into this third domain that the religious community falls. As we have seen, it is already engaged in protesting the conventional views of globalization in a surprising variety of ways and places. It is working both domestically and around the globe, employing a wide variety of strategies, building alliances with organizations both local and national, and creating in many cases new forms of ministry. By and large this religious activism is not yet very visible in the priorities of our mainstream religious bodies or church organizations, but exists in abundance just below the radar, and is gaining more visibility each year.

It is well beyond the scope of this book to offer a comprehensive list of these efforts. In this chapter I give only a sampling of the activities I've learned about, in which churches and other religious bodies are involved. It seems convenient to group these involvements into three categories: (1) actions seen as local but having global implications, (2) specific national or international campaigns in which church people are responding to some aspect of globalization, and (3) national or international gatherings of church bodies on an ecumenical level that are exploring globalization in depth and calling for church involvement.

Local Religious Engagements with Global Implications

It's understandable that economic justice projects at the local level may not relate their work to globalization issues. That doesn't mean that such work is not addressing globalization; it means that those involved may not have consciously interpreted their actions as an important local component of the wider global picture. How do you know whether your local project or program "qualifies" as an engagement that has global economic ramifications? I suggest three criteria: First, your program does not primarily offer a service to people (although it may contain that aspect). That is, the program is not primarily a charity work but a justice project. That means that, second, the program explicitly works to build increased power — clout — to the community and its working people. Third, the program action challenges or confronts local economic and political power held by corporations or companies or the government, and — an important "and" — they resist your action, precisely because it poses a challenge to their own power. This does not mean that you cannot have dialogue or negotiations with business or government; it just means that you must be aware of what is going on that relates to power, and that you are primarily about the business of empowerment for those who have little or no power. Sociologist Saskia Sassen says that "we learn something about power through its absence, and by moving through or negotiating the powers and terrains that connect powerlessness to power."[3]

Here are three examples of economic justice efforts that qualify as local manifestations of the global economic transformation that is reaching down into our communities:

The Kill-Floor Rebellion[4]

Omaha, Nebraska, is a prime center of the American meatpacking industry. Within the last two decades the city has seen a huge demographic shift toward Mexican and Central American immigrants, who now dominate the city's meatpacking plants. Spanish is now the language on the floor of almost every packing plant in the city; local radio stations play Spanish norteña and banda music. Largely preceding this demographic shift from south (below the Mexican border) to north (the United States and Canada) another shift occurred in the 1980s and '90s: a major restructuring of the meatpacking industry along with plant closures — a classic symptom of the new globalization then getting under way.[5] For the industry's new immigrant workers in Omaha the change meant low wages, oppressive working conditions, and many on-the-job injuries in this dangerous work of cutting, sawing, and packing beef carcasses.

Enter Father Damian Zuerlein and St. Agnes Catholic Church of Omaha, a parish home to hundreds of Latino workers at the local ConAgra beef plant. Early on, Father Damian had seen the plight of his new parishioners. A veteran activist and fluent in Spanish, he knew that the situation demanded a long-term strategy, one involving four groups working together: the workers, the meatpackers' union, the community, and the church. It took several years and some early failures to build a successful organizing strategy to support the ConAgra workers in their desire for fair working conditions and a union. But in the spring of 2002 at the Sunday mass at St. Agnes, a pivotal turning point came. Hundreds of packinghouse workers listened as the priest gave his homily in support of the workers; then he introduced Olga Espinosa, a "kill floor" worker at the plant. She described the hardships and indignities she and others had endured and the accidents she'd seen in her eight years on the floor, and then she issued an ultimatum: "I want everybody to stand up who's for the union," she asked. Slowly, in response to her call, and feeling the moral and spiritual support of the church behind them, the workers at the mass stood up. The following week, braving the intimidation and harassment of the plant management, the ConAgra workers voted to join the union, and they won.

The Naugatuck Valley Project

Once said to be one of the most industrialized places on earth, the Naugatuck River Valley in Connecticut began in the 1980s to suffer the same deindustrialization that was afflicting Omaha and other major industrial cities across America at that time. Factories closed, neighborhoods deteriorated, people left, and water and land polluted by industrial wastes was left to fester. But in 1983 a coalition of religious congregations, labor, small business, and tenant organizations came together to create jobs and affordable housing, clean up the environment, and maintain critical public and private services in the Valley. More than that, it redeveloped one industry and organized white- and blue-collar employees in three successful employee buyouts. Still going strong, it has fostered a number of significant environmental, jobs, community, and housing projects. "Our recent experience with organizing large public actions and addressing important and complex issues facing our communities has rekindled a sense of spiritual power — the understanding that groups of people acting upon their faith have the ability to change the world," says a Project description. But it warns: "The Valley's cities, suburbs, and undeveloped areas are at grave risk because of policies and decisions about development that grow out of a worldview that is both unrealistic and greedy: market extremism."[6]

In other words, the new global economy.

Clergy and Laity United for Economic Justice (CLUE)

By the mid-1990s in Los Angeles, the deepening poverty of the working poor — overwhelmingly people of color and mostly women — could no longer be denied even by people who were not paying that much attention. Its sharp contrast with the over twenty-one hundred new millionaires created in Los Angeles in the 1990s, for example, focused a light on the rapidly rising wealth of people at the other end of the scale, and underlined L.A. as an American Third World city. So when a handful of community and labor leaders went to some key Los Angeles Jewish and Christian clergy in late 1995 to invite them to become a major component of a campaign to pass a living wage ordinance in the city, the religious leaders, led by James M. Lawson Jr., a Methodist pastor and close colleague of Dr. Martin Luther King Jr., not only agreed but went a step further. The plight of the working poor in our communities will not be solved just by passing a living wage, they said. We need to organize a prophetic and strategic long-term response to economic injustice, they said. The result was the organizing of CLUE (of which I am an early member), which plunged full bore into the living wage campaign, organizing large numbers of clergy and laypeople, and closely coordinating its activities with the Los Angeles Living Wage Coalition. After eighteen months, the City Council of Los Angeles passed the living wage ordinance in spite of fierce business and press opposition, widespread prediction of failure, and a veto by the mayor of Los Angeles. Without a doubt, the religious community's participation was a decisive factor.

For the clergy and laypeople participating in this campaign the experience was transforming. Finding ourselves literally alongside the workers on whose behalf we worked affected us deeply. It kindled our admiration for what they endure in the workplace, especially their courage in standing up at great risk of losing their jobs. Just as important, this commitment put us shoulder to shoulder with a new wave of progressive union leaders, men and women (usually minorities) who are passionate for the cause of worker justice, and highly skilled in organizing. And it put us in contact with our elected leaders: to persuade them, to praise them when they did the right thing, and to try to understand them when they did not. Since then, CLUE (Web site: *www.cluela.org*) has built strongly upon these experiences and relationships, forming alliances with organized labor and involving itself deeply in the struggles of hotel workers, nursing home workers, janitors, airport workers, and most recently in 2004, grocery workers in their long and bitter strike in California. Currently CLUE has three full-time staff and the active support of about three hundred clergy, two dozen congregations, and several prominent religious leaders in the Los Angeles area.

In the three foregoing examples of local involvement, no explicit connections were made with the issues of the new globalization. But the recognition that existing economic power and public policies need to be confronted, and countervailing community and worker power built, was the cornerstone of each of the projects I've presented. And insofar as these and similar organizing projects are successful, they begin to chip away at the power of the larger forces of the global economic order. A next step with these projects would be to reflect on how their work might make a conscious programmatic link with the global networks and strategies emerging in the new global civil society.

Participating in Specific Globalization Campaigns at the Local Level

Three of the best-known campaigns in the United States and the developed world are the antisweatshop campaigns, the campaign to promote Fair Trade coffee, and the Slow Food movement. The extremely oppressive working conditions and low wages under which many garment workers labor, especially in Asia and Latin America but also here at home — who sew or manufacture such well-known brand-name products as Disney, Nike, Reebok, Gap, Old Navy, and others — have been widely publicized for several years. Church social-action groups and some religious congregations have joined with concerned citizens, college students, and unions in both legislative strategies and product boycotts aimed at pressuring companies to live up to established fair labor standards.

There is a wealth of information available on many current anti-sweatshop campaigns. One good starting place is the Web site of Global Exchange (*globalexchange.org/campaigns/sweatshops*). Following the principle that the best motivator to action occurs when church people meet workers and hear their stories, the National Labor Committee (Web site: *www.nlc.org*) has brought garment workers from as far away as Bangladesh to tell their stories to U.S. religious and community groups. The highly successful publicity generated by these encounters, together with letters written to legislators and the press has resulted in improved working conditions at targeted factories overseas, forcing compliance with labor law. But we should be reminded that such actions take only a small bite out of the ongoing global problem of sweatshop worker exploitation, and that this is in turn but a slice, although a highly visible one, of the global labor market. Furthermore, the targeted companies frequently adjust only to the extent they are pressured. If the spotlight moves elsewhere, they may revert to business as usual, or simply move their production if the heat becomes too great. That said, this does not diminish the importance of antisweatshop campaigns, which greatly aid in building public awareness as well as alleviating specific worker exploitation.

The campaign to buy Fair Trade coffee is similarly gaining wide participation. It is directed toward improving the lot of agricultural workers in developing countries. In coffee-growing countries many small farmers are offered prices for their coffee that are less than the costs of production, either driving them out of business or locking them into debt and poverty. In response to this situation, the "Fair Trade Labeling Organization International" was created, grouping together nonprofit organizations from seventeen countries to reach out to such coffee growers. It confers the Fair Trade label on qualifying coffee growers, which are frequently small farmer co-operatives. An importer of such coffee must agree to pay farmers a minimum price per pound (at this writing, $1.26), provide them credit, and offer technical assistance such as help to make the transition to organic farming. Among others, Global Exchange (look under "campaigns" on their Web site) is a wide advertiser and resource for the campaign, and works with a network of student, social justice, religious, environmental, and economic justice groups to urge, for example, that colleges purchase Fair Trade coffee. Likewise, churches and church organizations are joining the campaign. My own church promotes Fair Trade coffee through its Episcopal Relief and Development agency (the Episcopalians, with a bit of ecclesiastical swagger, call theirs "Bishops Blend").

A movement related to the Fair Trade coffee movement is the Slow Food Movement, originating in Rome in 1986, and now worldwide. It works to promote the food traditions that are part of the cultural identity of the country. It emphasizes biodiversity, caring for the land, and locally and organically grown foods, and it has educational and public outreach programs. In the United States there are 150 chapters, or *convivia*, as they are called (Web site: *www.slowfoodusa.org*).

Linking Churches with Immigrant Workers

Instead of bringing workers to the churches, as the National Labor Committee does, the interfaith Borderlinks project (see their Web site at *www.borderlinks.org*) brings church people to the workers. Based in Tucson, Arizona, it has conducted overseas travel seminars in which people from the wealthy North and the impoverished global South come together. More geographically accessible and having great impact are Borderlinks' conducted group visits to the Mexican border at Nogales, south of Tucson. In these visits people of faith, surrounded by the arid Southwest desert where so many migrants have died trying to enter the United States, dialogue with workers, recent immigrants, immigration agents, and other officials. They seek to understand the implications of the global economy for the immigrants, and for residents and communities on both sides of the border. Such visits can be life-transforming for church folk.

Immigrant Workers Freedom Ride

Inspired by the Freedom Riders of the civil rights movement of the 1960s, almost a thousand immigrant workers representative not only of Latin American countries but of Asia and Africa as well, together with religious and union leaders, boarded buses departing from ten cities across the United States in August 2003. Supported by organized labor and a large number of national and local religious bodies, they headed for Washington, D.C., to push for federal legislation to legalize their status, have a clear road to citizenship, reunify their families, and have a voice on the job. En route, the buses stopped in 106 cities, often being hosted by religious groups organized by the National Interfaith Committee for Worker Justice (now Interfaith Worker Justice). After their Washington visits with members of Congress, over 150,000 immigrants and supporters gathered in New York City for a rally and celebration. Hundreds of newspaper articles were written about their journey, including six feature articles by the *New York Times*. Said one leader of the event: "It gave ordinary immigrants the opportunity to be subjects in the debate rather than the objects of it." In a time when it is increasingly difficult to awaken the public to the plight of forgotten and marginalized people, it becomes crucial to look for new and imaginative ways to gain public attention; this pilgrimage for justice was outstanding in that regard.

It's important to underline here the connection that immigration and immigrants have with the realities of the new global economy, for it is easy to dismiss the influx of immigrants to this country and to other wealthy nations as just a matter of wanting to find "greener grass on the other side." But it is the worsening poverty in poor nations that increasingly pushes workers to leave their homes and go anywhere to survive. Moreover it is the immigrant workforce already in America, and spreading throughout the country, that usually takes the lowest-paid jobs available — and then frequently finds the door largely shut to upward mobility. That, of course, is precisely a hallmark of the new globalization.

Sustainable World

All Saints Church, a large Episcopal church with a progressive social tradition located in Pasadena, California, developed a multifaceted study and action program on globalization after an extensive small-group study of David Korten's book *The Post-Corporate World*. The church has been the prime mover in two major regional conferences on globalization, each drawing three hundred to four hundred people to hear economists, religious leaders, social scientists, and grassroots activists analyze the issues and strategize for action. In addition to recruiting people to go on Borderlinks trips, taking a fact-finding trip to Guatemala to understand better the impact of globalization on Guatemalan women, Sustainable World urges that its members be active participants in support of the working poor in the Los Angeles area, especially through CLUE (see foregoing pages). The group is also an active promoter of antisweatshop activities and Fair Trade coffee. Recently it has begun holding seminars on socially responsible investing.

National and International Gatherings of Churches Exploring Globalization

You might think that apart from the occasional pronouncements and resolutions coming from our denominational leaders and national church conventions, the involvements by church people noted in the previous pages constitute essentially the thrust of engagement by the churches on the globalization issue: a few pronouncements at the top, a good amount of activity on the part of religious activists, an activist church here and there, and that's about it. It is a welcome surprise, therefore, to find that a whole range of conferences, discussions, consultations, and encounters focusing on the new global economy is going on across continents under the auspices of national, international, and ecumenical church bodies. For example,

in 2003, two consultations were held between staff members of the
World Council of Churches, the World Bank, and the International
Monetary Fund — both of these at the initiative of the World Bank
and the IMF — on the subject of trade policies as they affect developing nations. Another consultation, Moved by God's Spirit, met in
Bossey, Switzerland, in November 2003, and worked at clarifying different ways to speak theologically about the churches' engagement
with the global economy. This consultation, of the Orthodox, Anglican, Lutheran, and Reformed churches, was part of an ongoing
process initiated by the World Council of Churches' 1998 Assembly. And in early 2004, Catholic Relief Services USA was proceeding
to set up conferences around the country to focus on the regional
manifestations of globalization. Also, in January 2004 more than
a hundred leaders and grassroots participants from the Americas
were gathered by Church World Service and the Canadian Council of Churches in Stony Point, New York, to discuss international
trade issues vital to this hemisphere, and to issue a plan of action.
Said participant Karen Bloomquist of the Lutheran World Federation: "Globalization... raises the importance of empowering moral
agency and 'moral nerve' to change what is occurring."

So what are these groups discussing? In a word, trade.[7] The unfair
arrangements that currently dictate the conduct of international trade
appear to be the overwhelming concern of these church gatherings,
reflecting accurately the strong concerns of poor and marginalized
people in developing countries. At Stony Point, for example, the
conference of North American church leaders reported on NAFTA's
negative impact on people and the environment as a result of its trade
policies. Following its declaration "For Just Trade in the Service of
an Economy of Life," the conference issued a detailed plan of action
to serve as a guide for denominations and church agencies. The plan
ranges from developing a trade policy advocacy strategy aimed at the
U.S. and Canadian governments, to preparing resources for churches,
such as study guides and worship aids. For further information see the
Web site: *www.churchworldservice.org/news/archives/2004/01/157.*

Another ecumenical conference in early 2004 gathered representatives from eight Latin American countries plus the United States
and Canada in Havana, Cuba, to protest the proposed Free Trade
Area of the Americas treaty (FTAA), calling it "an imperial pretext
to annex Latin America through the institutionalization of a cultural,
military, and economic system of domination." It also specifically
warned against the incursion of conservative religious movements
and churches that "through a theological fundamentalism support
a neoliberal ideology . . . aimed at undermining [authentic] Christian
ecumenism."[8]

The fact that the World Bank and the International Monetary Fund
invited the World Council of Churches to meet to discuss globalization issues is an indication that they are not immune to public opinion
regarding their policies and activities. It is further proof that when it
chooses to exercise its moral authority, the religious community can
have influence. That said, according to one religious participant[9] a
big question for the church representatives taking part in this dialogue is whether the IMF and the World Bank will really be able to
move away from the neoliberal paradigm — a strong concern shared
by Joseph Stiglitz in his book *Globalization and Its Discontents*. All
at the conferences, according to participant Pamela Brubaker, agreed
upon the principles of the U.N.'s Millennium Development Goals, but
the two international trade institutions maintained that "we must not
undermine the international banking system."

That system, it is clear, is close to the heart of the contentions
between the haves and have-nots of the world. Nonetheless, the two
trade groups in these encounters with the World Council of Churches
did admit to some mistakes in the past and committed to continue
the dialogue.

To sum up this chapter's glimpse into the responses of the churches
to the new globalization: we can be very heartened by the wide range
of activities, the sophistication of much of the economic analysis, and
the collaboration both across religious boundaries, and also with secular groups. I emphasize again that this list is but a random sampling
of what I've found to be going on. I have not mentioned the many

books recently beginning to pour forth on the subject of globalization and economic justice from the pens of Christian academics. Particularly impressive in both the activism and the scholarly efforts is the new willingness of the churches to directly criticize the current workings of the global economic system, including strong critiques of capitalism. As we have seen, neoliberal economics in particular — the ascendancy of capitalist ideology in national government policy, and in international trade and financial organizations — is named and denounced in several church critiques. Looking back a decade or so, say to the early 1990s, it would be hard to find such a willingness to directly criticize global capitalism coming from Christian leaders in the developed world. It has to be the increasingly apparent global crisis acting as a persistent prick upon the consciousness of Christians — in much the same way the American churches in the 1880s and 1890s were finally stirred into action by the injustices borne by U.S. industrial workers of that time — that has begun to awaken us.

But our list of involvements and accomplishments has its weaknesses. Chief among them is how few of the actions, boycotts, protests, conferences, and pronouncements carried out by church people have percolated down to the level of church congregations becoming involved *as congregations*. It still appears to be overwhelmingly the case that priests and pastors are not yet putting themselves on the line in sermons, prayers, and programs that address the evils of globalization. A related weakness is how so little news of the impressive and sophisticated critiques and recommendations of some of the national and international church bodies mentioned here filters down to congregational level. One has to conclude that the top religious leaders of our several denominations have yet to raise their voices to decibel levels sufficient to reach down and disturb our churches with the holy fire of the God of justice and peace. Finally, as evidenced by the World Council of Churches meeting in November 2003, cited earlier in this chapter, the theological approaches of the different church bodies to the issue of globalization, and also our approaches to the religious beliefs of our co-religionists in the other major world faiths remain very much at an elementary level.

For Reflection and Discussion

1. This chapter lists three categories of activities the churches have been involved in, in their responses to globalization: local, national or international, and international religious gatherings. Pick one activity from each category, discuss, and brainstorm on how your church or community might become similarly involved.

2. How can we bridge the gap between the considerable activity to address globalization that is going on at national and international levels, and the lack of awareness of this activity at local church levels? What specific actions to improve awareness might be taken?

3. How do we in the churches begin to think theologically about globalization issues? How do we apply our theological thinking to economic and global justice?

Chapter Thirteen

Another World Is Possible

Organizing and Theologizing

Before every human being there walks an angel proclaiming, "Make way, make way for the image of God!"
— Rabbinic saying

The victims of globalization can ... be its means of redemption, and without making them central to the debate there will never be a human globalization.
— Jon Sobrino, *Redeeming Globalization through Its Victims*

Globalization is imposing new ways of "being church," affecting even the church's self-understanding. ... The first thing to do is to move from a static to a dynamic concept of church.
— H. H. Aram I, Catholicos of Cilicia, Armenian Orthodox Church

I T'S NOT EASY to get a group going on the globalization issue in the local church. How do you start a dialogue on the subject? Even among parishioners who see social justice as an essential component of the Christian gospel the barriers are substantial. Add to this the protestation that globalization as an issue is "too far out there — we have more urgent issues closer to home." Moreover, it's an immensely complex issue (point ceded!), one dealing with economics and — the dreaded "p" word — politics. Perhaps most threatening of all, when you start questioning some of the tenets of modern-day capitalism, you are "touching the ark," which in the mythology of ancient Israel could cause death (1 Sam. 6:6). But inexorably, over against this defensive reaction the realization grows that our world has become increasingly and irrevocably joined in a common destiny: bound together socially, economically, and environmentally. Again, William Greider's book title captures it: *One World, Ready or Not.* The good news for us as people of faith is that recent years have seen a remarkable blossoming of church responses, even if not much yet at the congregational level.

In chapter 10, "*Oikonomia* and the Global Household," I looked for a fresh way to connect the new global realities with our religious tradition, and suggested that the Global Household can be a metaphor for our new millennium world, one that through the eyes of our faith corresponds to Jesus' vision of the kingdom of God. My own Anglican tradition finds the doctrine of the Incarnation of Christ to be expressive of a new reality: the coming of Christ to earth as transformative not just for believing Christians, but also for the entire human race: the whole realm of visible and invisible worlds mystically brought into close and inseparable union.[1] Other Christian traditions apply our biblical and historical heritage with similar and equally valid formulations. Moreover, the other major faiths arrive at similar perspectives — witness the rabbinic saying, "Make way, make way for the image of God" quoted at the head of this chapter.

A central thesis of this book is the relevance not only of the Holy Scriptures but of the whole weight of the Christian tradition in the claim that the social and economic realities of all human life, including economics itself, are the legitimate concerns of our faith. So our task in "reclaiming lost ground" is twofold: to reclaim our historic heritage as an undergirding of the comprehensiveness of the Christian faith, and to organize in our churches for action.

Reclaiming Our Religious Heritage

In chapter 2 of this book I sought to give a brief glimpse into the richness of our Christian tradition through the centuries, a glimpse I followed up more substantively in later chapters. I chose three themes: work, poverty, and *oikonomia* — the Global Household — through which the interplay of our religious traditions and the evolution of the economic order in history might be seen. For example, we saw that the medieval church included the redemption of the whole social and economic order as a legitimate concern, and that this conviction was based upon both the Bible and the writings of the early church fathers. We also saw that notwithstanding the rise of an ethos of individualism in the Reformation, movements embodying a holistic concept of justice remained alive in the churches. In chapter 4 I described significant movements in France, England, and the United States after World War II that attempted to explore the industrial world of work and relate it to Christian faith. Although these attempts in Industrial Mission, as it was called, were largely a failure, they nonetheless represented a serious attempt by the churches to address directly the modern industrial system itself as a legitimate moral concern.

Half a century earlier, at the turn of the nineteenth century, the churches had awakened to the injustices inflicted upon the industrial working class and the widening gap between rich and poor in America. The social gospel movement that followed was not only theological but manifested itself in the activities of many churches and clergy in support of working people. Prominent clerical leaders were making radical analyses that find surprising echo in today's globalization debate. Wrote James O. S. Huntington (founder of the Anglican Order of the Holy Cross), an activist labor priest in New York City about a hundred years ago: "No one can doubt what work lies before us. It is the building of a new world.... A horde of slaves cannot make a free state until they cease to be slaves. A hundred blind men cannot combine into a seeing fellowship. The edifice of a generous democracy cannot be raised on the basis of materialism and self-interest."[2] Not a bad challenge for today!

Moving to the twentieth century, in chapter 7 we saw some signs of church engagement with the larger issues of economic exploitation developing as far back as 1970 — the precursors of the new globalization. Chapter 8 documented the awakening of the churches in the 1980s and 1990s to its moral implications. In this period we began to see various national church bodies make resolutions and issue position papers that were seriously critical of the direction of the new global economic order. Even more important, the churches joined with other movements to launch the Jubilee 2000 campaign to address the huge debt burden being placed on poor countries; this international campaign experienced marked success. Chapter 9, focusing on the working poor in the global economy, asserted that for the churches they are the linchpin to the globalization debate.

How can we take what we have learned, and of course will go on learning, about the new global economy and about our rich religious tradition, that can speak strongly to the issue and begin to think theologically about it? Can we begin to envision, even if only dimly, a "theology of globalization"? Even raising the question sounds pretentious at this point. What we can do is identify some theological points of departure that can serve as a foundation. Foremost would be the liberation theologies coming to the fore in the last half of the last century. From Latin America, from black and feminist theologians, and from ecological theologies of liberation we are provided both with the perspective of Jesus' own "preferential option for the poor"[3] in the Scriptures, and that of the victims of economic and social oppression. They help save us from viewing the world, and our theologies, through the lens of Western affluence and privilege. In this regard, we are slow to absorb the fact that by 2050 only about one-fifth of the world's estimated 3 billion Christians will be non-Hispanic whites. Those of us who are white, particularly white males, must clearly become radically open to new perspectives.

In addition to beginning to formulate a Christian theological position on globalization, we need to acquaint ourselves with the views of the other great world religions — Judaism, the Muslim faith, Buddhism, Hinduism — to find common spiritual ground to confront the injustices of globalization. Each of these religious traditions has a universal vision of unity. Another interesting fact — one worth pondering when you apply it to the current global economic order — is that they all agree that greed is not an admirable human trait![4]

Christians are understandably more acquainted with Jewish global perspectives, in particular the message of universalism encountered in the book of Isaiah, the Psalms, and elsewhere in the Old Testament.[5] Also, going beyond Israel's own religion to the universal, one rabbinic principle, *tikkun olam*, the healing of the world, has found special relevance beyond Judaism, in Christian circles.

In Islam, the proclamation of the unity of God is especially strong: "Allah is one, and is the Cherisher and Sustainer of the worlds," as Ameer Ali, an Islamic economist, reminds us.[6]

In precapitalist civilizations, as with Christianity, Islam viewed economics and economic development as subsumed under the paramount objective of human development. Islam as a religion is not against the profit motive, says Ali, but it is not willing to allow the profit motive to determine human progress. That strong statement clearly puts it in substantive conflict with the current direction of globalization.

In Buddhism (as in the other religions) the Buddha's essential teachings do not address or endorse any one economic system; the Buddha's teaching moves almost entirely on another plane. Nonetheless, in Buddhism greed is a major part of the root cause of suffering. Thich Nhat Hanh, the Vietnamese Buddhist widely known and admired in the West, has joined a socialist perspective to his Buddhist one, and has developed the term "interbeing": to be in this world is to "inter-be."[7]

In Hinduism, which lacks any well-defined ecclesiastical organization, kinship is the essential religious element. The Vedas (the oldest scriptures of Hinduism) teach that the whole of creation, including the human family, originates with God, a belief obviously echoed in the Judeo-Christian story of Adam and Eve.

Not surprisingly, as is the case with Christianity, so also within each of the other world religions, a variety of perspectives can be found to exist regarding the globalization of the economy. This said, it is clear that we have common ground. Writes Chandra Muzaffar in the summary chapter of *Subverting Greed*: "The similarities are so overwhelming that one can talk with some confidence about the religions evolving a shared universal moral and spiritual ethic vis-à-vis the global economy. However, for such an ethic to evolve, we have to go beyond our present endeavor. . . . These traditions have not as yet really dialogued with one another."[8]

I believe there are four overarching global realities that the world's great religions must take into account in any quest to articulate a theology adequate to the new global economic realities: The market as God, the emergence of the market state, the United States as the new world imperial power, and the bias of a Western perspective on globalization.

First, *the market as God.* In chapter 10 and previously, I've alluded to the coronation of capitalism, especially in the United States, as the sole remaining economic ideology following the fall of communism. Theologian Harvey Cox, deciding several years ago on a friend's advice to read the business pages of the daily newspapers to find out what was really going on, tells of making a surprising discovery, namely, that his reading of the *Wall Street Journal* and other periodicals revealed a striking resemblance to the book of Genesis, the Epistle to the Romans, and St. Augustine's *City of God.* "Behind descriptions of market reforms, monetary policy and the convolutions of the Dow, I gradually made out the pieces of a grand narrative about the inner meaning of human history, why things had gone wrong, and how to put them right," writes Cox. "Theologians call these myths of origin, legends of the fall, and doctrines of sin and redemption. But here they were again, and in only thin disguise: chronicles about the creation of wealth, the seductive temptations of statism, captivity to faceless economic cycles, and ultimately, salvation of free markets."[9]

One fears to touch the Ark; yet as the Old Testament prophets did relentlessly, the "idol" of global capitalism must be named and dethroned as must any false gods.

Second, *the emergence of the market state.* Related to the evolution of the market as God is the evolution of the market state, and the corresponding weakening of the power of the nation-state. Government's responsibility to "promote the general welfare," as the Preamble to our Constitution says, is evolving in the new global order to a very different function. According to Philip Bobbitt, the function of the new market state is now mainly to clear a space for individuals or groups to do their own negotiating, to secure the best deal or the best value for money in pursuing what they want.[10] In other words, government is "dumbed down" to serve mainly as a broker for economic agreements; responsibility for the "general welfare" of the people is relegated to the back burner. One hopes that the announcement of the death of the nation-state is premature at this juncture in history. The requirement that governments accept basic responsibility for the welfare of their people must be vigorously reasserted.

The third area for the religious community to understand and address is *the emergence of the United States as the new imperial power.* On September 17, 2002, one year after the catastrophic terrorist attack upon the United States, our government issued a defining political document: *The National Security Strategy of the United States of America.* Its introductory statement, over the signature of President Bush himself, opens with this sentence: "The great struggles of the twentieth century between liberty and totalitarianism ended with a decisive victory for the forces of freedom — *and a single sustainable model for national success: freedom, democracy, and free enterprise"* [emphasis added]. It affirmed this formula as valid for all people and "across the ages," going on to say that "today the U.S. enjoys a position of unparalleled military strength and great economic and political influence."[11] "We will actively work to bring the hope of democracy, development, free markets, and free trade to every corner of the world," the introduction adds. In its section titled "Ignite a New Era of Global Economic Growth through Free Markets and Free Trade," the National Security Strategy document unequivocally puts the weight of American economic policy behind the policies promoted by the IMF, NAFTA, and the WTO — policies we've seen to be broadly averse to the wider goals of human development for all people. Distorting history, it baldly asserts that "the concept of free trade arose as a moral principle even before it became a pillar of economics"[12] — an assertion that would have astonished the Christian theologians and canon law compilers who shaped the social ethics of the medieval period and before, not to mention other historians.

It thus becomes clear that the great and complex issues of globalization cannot be effectively addressed without also challenging the sweeping new hegemonic policies so clearly staked out recently by the United States. And we should add that such policies may well remain essentially in place in the near future regardless of whether Republicans or Democrats are in power.

Fourth, *the bias of a Western perspective on globalization.* Writes Amartya Sen: "There is a nicely stylized history in which the great developments happened in Europe: First came the Renaissance, then the Enlightenment and the Industrial Revolution, and these led to a massive increase in living standards in the West. And now the great achievements of the West are spreading to the world. In this view, globalization is not only good, it is also a gift from the West to the world." We have to be suspicious of a pro-Western chauvinism in many contemporary writings, he adds: "While the achievements of modern technology have resulted in undeniable progress, the principal challenge relates to inequality.... The troubling inequalities include disparities in affluence and also to gross asymmetries in political, social and economic opportunities and power" both between nations and within nations.[13]

Organizing for Action

Most religious slogans, even good ones, are apt only for a short time, then fade away. An exception, one relevant for us as we address the new global economic order, is "Think Globally, Act Locally": strikingly pertinent today after being around for several decades. It underlines the imperative for never losing in our work an awareness of the connectedness of the local with the global, and also for constantly reexamining how the two are connected. For example, the issue of trade unexpectedly emerged in the 2004 presidential election in the United States, giving high visibility to the free trade–fair trade debate that has been moving to prominence at least since Seattle, 1999. Such a development might influence some action strategies under consideration by the churches, perhaps opening up new ways to respond.

As the previous pages have indicated, we have an imperative to be interfaith not only in dialogue together, but in our action strategies if we are to be at all effective. It should be clear by now that

Presbyterian, or Lutheran, or Episcopal or Catholic responses are by themselves totally inadequate to the task. Moreover, such interfaith endeavors must join in partnership with the secular community. In the words of one British theologian, we in the religious community are now in the "new secular age of partnerships," representing a growing recognition at all levels of our global context that the complexity of problems we now face means that no one discipline can explain them effectively, and no one sector, public or private, can engage them effectively.[14]

I won't detail here the steps for organizing, say, a group on globalization within a church; basic group organizing principles are well known in churches, and in any case organizing manuals and guides are widely available for these mundane but essential steps.[15] Instead I want to pose four questions that should be fundamental starting points for any organizing effort on globalization, questions we must continue to check in with at every juncture of our work. They may seem elementary, but the consistency and thoroughness of their asking will go far toward determining a successful outcome of any strategy.

The first question is: *Where is the pain?* That is, where are people and their communities hurting (there is a lot to choose from!)? Obviously, since the global scene is our "household," the question pertains to both near and far, from Filipino corn farmers to sweatshop workers in Honduras, to immigrant janitors and hotel workers in Boston and Los Angeles, and beyond. And what, exactly, is the hurt? For example, is it low wages, exploitation at work, lack of work (due, for example, to the inability to sell a vital crop on the world market), lack of land, lack of life-saving drugs (as in the AIDS pandemic), etc.?

Second, *Why is this happening?* What particular public policies, corporate practices, or other influences are the leading or contributing causes of the particular situation under discussion? There are obvious culprits on the global scene that might be identifiable: the current policies of the international financial and trade organizations (IMF, NAFTA, WTO, FTAA); our own agricultural policies that severely hinder poor farmers overseas; current investment and tax policies; or some of the others I've mentioned in this book. In such areas, there are frequently impacts felt on our local scene that may provide opportunities for involvement. If a local issue is decided upon as a focus, prevailing local political and economic policies and business practices are usually causes that need to be addressed. As we have said, such policies are usually widespread around the country. In modern-day America, urban economic policies and practices invariably are tilted toward favoring large developers and their economic interests. Whether a particular development proposal will create not only jobs, but living wage jobs, affirm the right to organize, preserve the neighborhood, safeguard the environment, and generally enhance the social well-being of all the people in the community: these are the conditions we in the churches should be organizing to fight for. Furthermore, these questions are globalization questions. They have to do with how political and economic power are used to truly benefit human development. So churches that work on this level are doing "globalization work"; they are an authentic part of the larger global push to humanize and transform the global economic order. It should be obvious, then, that the policies of municipal city councils invariably have much to do with these issues, and themselves should become a focus for action.

Third, in assessing the possibilities for action, whether locally or beyond, we need to ask, *Who might our allies be, not only in the wider religious community, but in the community at large.* What groups or coalitions are out there that we could link up with — community action groups, labor unions, small farmers, sympathetic politicians, academic researchers — who have focused on concerns similar to ones we have identified? Here I want to stress first and foremost the need to travel. By that I mean the necessity of going across town (or even just a few blocks), or across the country, or the globe where possible, to acquire a first-hand acquaintance with the people for whom we would be advocates. In so doing, we will discover that those who are the "victims" of the injustice do not need our help in setting their agenda; they know better than anyone else what their situation is. They are the primary actors and protagonists in building a new world. Our role is to find out, in being alongside them and in listening to them, how we can support them as sisters and brothers.

Fourth, *how can we become proficient at economic and social analysis?* Oppression has economic and political roots. A project that does not take the time to analyze the roots of a particular situation and use the information effectively will find itself addressing the periphery of the problem, with little prospect for real change. The good news is that we church folk don't have to do this by ourselves; there are college and university economists and sociologists in almost every community who would be delighted to lend a hand (and it goes toward validating for them why they went into teaching!). The trade unions, especially the progressive ones, usually have excellent research departments. The need for such professional analysis becomes indispensable, for example, in campaigns to persuade elected officials to adopt positions favorable to real human empowerment. For national and overseas projects, there are many progressive nonprofit organizations whose research is available online — for example, Global Exchange, the Center for Economic and Policy Research, the Economic Policy Institute, and others (see Appendix, p. 195).

Finally, Things to Keep in Mind

Organize to win! Build from small victories to larger ones. We in the churches frequently become used to social action modes of operation that assume that a kind of "gesture for justice" is sufficient; i.e., we will "do our part," hope that others do theirs, and leave the rest to God. This mind-set is basically a cop-out: it is partly a result of our having experienced defeat in previous endeavors along the way, so much so that we "get used to it." The attitude reveals a serious spiritual failure on our part, a failure to take on the big challenges God offers us, a failure to dream big and to do what committed Christians through the ages have always done: to proceed as if God herself/himself is the engine for justice, that we are the hands of God in the world, and that God's love and justice will inevitably triumph. So we must design a campaign, and take part with others in campaigns that expect not merely to "make a statement" but to win a tangible victory. In campaigns in which I've participated in Los Angeles, I've been inspired by the workers of Local 11 of the hotel workers union, who at demonstrations and marches exude the spirit of winning — they and we chanting together, "Sí se puede!" (Yes, we can!) as they organize to win a new labor contract. And it is obvious that in Seattle, and in Cancún and Miami in 2003, the organizers believed — correctly — that they could really tilt the battle toward justice.

Winning requires long-term commitment. Setting a time line of three to five years for major goals is a must, and helps keep us focused. Setbacks are inevitable, but as we know, the struggle for peace and justice is not for the faint of heart.

Use to the max the moral authority of the church, and even better, that of the interfaith community. Such authority is not limited to ecclesiastical pronouncements by top religious leaders, although I have found that they are frequently willing to take a public stand if the moral and spiritual issues are explained to them, and if they feel that the issue has the involvement of at least some of their clergy and laity. There are various ways to use this moral authority effectively. For example, street theater or other symbolic actions that contain religious significance, singing, praying in various ways: all invest a protest or demonstration with a spiritual significance that is not lost on all those involved, and that carries the event beyond the purely political, authenticating the involvement of religious leaders. Also, very crucial to such actions is learning how to use the press as ally. For example, a large protest march of clergy and laypeople down Rodeo Drive in Beverly Hills left a plate of bitter herbs at one hotel refusing to sign a contract with the hotel workers, while another hotel that had just signed the contract got milk and honey — all well covered by the press.[16] So the forms of taking religious actions in support of the group or groups that are our concern are limited only by our imaginations.

To reclaim lost ground is, I believe, the challenge facing us who claim the Christian faith and are ready to engage the principalities and powers of the new global economic order. As we have looked at our own two-thousand-year tradition, I hope we can see that "the saints" in the church have many times traveled this path before us and have fought the good fight; that our present struggles, while new in detail and aspect, are essentially the same: against greed, injustice, and oppression — everything that dehumanizes; and that we can feel the saints' presence among us and be inspired by their example. And as we move toward solidarity with our brothers and sisters both at home and overseas who have been denied the chance to participate in the dream of basic human equality, let us be grateful that so many of them have nonetheless shown the way for us, and persisted in the dream of a world made new. Together with them we can reclaim the ground lost to injustice and oppression, and join in this great struggle, witnessing to the power of God working among us, in Isaiah's words, to

> loose the bonds of injustice,
> to undo the thongs of the yoke,
> to let the oppressed go free,
> and to break every yoke.
>
> —Isaiah 58

For Reflection and Discussion

1. Using some of the suggestions in this chapter, or your own intuition, begin to figure out how you will become engaged!

Appendix

A Brief List
of Selected Web Sites on
Globalization and Religious Involvement

Globalization

www.aflcio.org
> Web site of the AFL-CIO. Tracks and advocates for many issues
> related to the labor movement, workers, and economic justice.

www.cepr.net
> Center for Economic Policy and Research. Tracks economic issues
> domestic and global, and offers in-depth articles and analysis.

www.citizen.org/trade
> The "Global Trade Watch" of Public Citizen. Offers timely
> articles and alerts on global trade issues.

www.epinet.org
> Economic Policy Institute. A preeminent national research group
> focusing on labor and economic data, trade, and globalization.

www.faireconomy.org
> United for a Fair Economy. Excellent source of information.
> Raises awareness that concentrated wealth and power undermine
> the economy and corrupt democracy.

www.globalexchange.org
> Global Exchange. An excellent multipurpose Web site with much
> info on economic justice, trade, sweatshops, fair trade coffee and
> other products, etc.

www.labornotes.org
>   News of organized labor and workers in general. Current issues from a progressive perspective.

www.livingwagecampaign.org
>   Organized by ACORN. The most comprehensive info available on U.S. living wage campaigns, plus tips on how to organize a campaign.

www.slowfoodusa.org
>   USA-based component of an international movement aiming to restore and celebrate food traditions, and also to promote organic foods, sustainability, biodiversity, and local food sources.

Religious Involvement

www.allsaints-pas.org
>   All Saints Episcopal Church, Pasadena, California. Has a comprehensive and multifaceted program called Sustainable World that addresses globalization with education and action components. Has organized several large conferences on globalization topics.

www.borderlinks.org
>   Based in Arizona, Borderlinks runs direct education programs related to immigration issues on the U.S.-Mexican border and puts them in the wider context of globalization issues. Also organizes other trips.

www.Christian-aid.org.uk
>   British-based Christian Aid, a longtime international agency of the churches in the United Kingdom and Ireland, has been involved in trade issues and has an active trade justice campaign.

www.jubileeusa.org
>   Jubilee USA continues the work of the Jubilee 2000 campaign. Comprising churches, unions, and community groups, it is the best U.S. source for the "Drop the Debt" campaign, and the best source on global debt.

www.lutheranworld.org

> Web site of the Lutheran World Federation. Works closely with the World Council of Churches and the World Alliance of Reformed Churches in globalization issues. On the Web site, follow the link to economic globalization and human rights.

www.maryknoll.org

> At the Web site go to "Office for Global Concerns." Very good info and opportunities for involvement from this renowned Catholic Missionary Society.

www.nlc.org

> The National Labor Committee brings overseas garment workers to the United States to tell their stories to churches and others. A strong and effective advocate for fair wages and working conditions for garment workers.

www.sabbatheconomics.org

> The Sabbath Economics Collaborative is a national, membership-based network that facilitates cooperation and communication among theologians, economists, and activists who are exploring contemporary issues of faith and economic justice.

www.warc.ch/who.welcome

> The World Alliance of Reformed Churches includes Lutheran and other Reformed churches in the United States and Europe. It is an active partner with the World Council of Churches and the Lutheran World Federation. At the Web site, go to "covenanting for justice."

www.wcc-coe.org

> The World Council of Churches Web site. Go to *what/jpc.economy .html*. Its Justice, Peace and Creation link has a good introductory essay and helpful links to "economic globalization."

Notes

Foreword

1. Bernard Kent Markwell, *The Anglican Left: Radical Social Reformers in the Church of England and the Protestant Episcopal Church 1846–1954* (Brooklyn, N.Y.: Carlson, 1991).

2. John Oliver, *The Church and Social Order: Social Thought in the Church of England 1918–1939* (London: Mowbrays, 1968), 49.

3. Bruce Wollenberg, *Christian Social Thought in Great Britain between the Wars* (Lanham, Md.: University Press of America, 1997), 7.

4. William G. Robinson, "Globalisation: Nine Theses on Our Epoch," *Race and Class* 38, no. 2 (1996).

5. Although the term "Anglo-USA" is clumsy, I think that "Anglo-American" is dangerously confusing. The United States is a small part of North America, and an even smaller part of America as a whole. Christians who are committed by their faith to the pursuit of truth should stop using "America" and "American" as if they were synonymous with "the United States." This spiritual discipline would help to expose a major element of our current crisis.

Introduction

1. *Oikonomia* is the Greek word that is the root of the word "economy." In ancient Greece it meant the management of the household's valuable assets. It is used here to mean the global economy.

Chapter One / The New Globalization

1. Kent Wong et al., eds., *Teaching for Change: Popular Education and the Labor Movement* (Los Angeles: UCLA Center for Labor Research and Education, 2002).

2. *Ending the Race to the Bottom*, a report by the National Labor Committee, 2001. The average workweek for a woman garment worker at the Young An Hat factory is seventy-eight to eighty-five hours, with an average pay between thirteen and seventeen cents per hour.

3. Harvey Cox, "The Market as God," *Atlantic Monthly* (March 1999).

4. William Greider, *One World, Ready or Not: The Manic Logic of Global Capitalism* (New York: Touchstone Books, 1997), 11.

5. Tina Rosenberg, "The Free-Trade Fix" *New York Times Magazine*, August 18, 2002.

6. Special issue on globalism, *The American Prospect* (Winter 2002).

7. Saskia Sassen, *Cities in a World Economy*, 2nd ed. (Thousand Oaks, Calif.: Pine Forge Press, 2000), 4.

8. United for a Fair Economy, *The Growing Divide: Inequality and the Roots of Economic Insecurity* (Boston: United for a Fair Economy, November 2001).

9. Sassen, *Cities in a World Economy*, 6.

10. Kevin Phillips, *Arrogant Capital* (Boston: Little, Brown, 1994), 84 (emphasis in original). His new book, *Wealth and Democracy* (New York: Broadway Books, 2002), further develops this subject. See also my chapter 10.

11. Sassen, *Cities in a World Economy*, 28.

12. Thomas L. Friedman, *The Lexus and the Olive Tree*, rev. ed. (New York: Anchor Books, 2000).

13. Ibid., 102–10.

14. Naomi Klein, *No Logo: Taking Aim at the Brand Bullies* (New York: Picador USA, 2000), 21.

15. Margaret Talbot, "Why, Isn't He Just the Cutest Brand-Image Enhancer You've Ever Seen?" *New York Times Magazine*, September 21, 2003.

16. Benjamin R. Barber, *Jihad vs. McWorld* (New York: Ballantine Books, 1996), 128.

17. The Women's Christian Temperance Movement broadened its focus from an initial concern with alcoholism to women's suffrage and other issues of social reform.

18. Interview with Naomi Klein in the *Los Angeles Times*, April 29, 2001.

Chapter Two / Christian Social Commitment

1. William Temple, *Christianity and Social Order* (1942; repr. New York: Seabury Press, 1977), 29.

2. Theodore Roosevelt, *The Foes of Our Own Household* (New York: George H. Doran, 1917), 226.

3. Henry F. May, *Protestant Churches and Industrial America* (New York: Harper and Brothers, 1949), 173.

4. John C. Cort, *Christian Socialism* (Maryknoll, N.Y.: Orbis, 1988), 47.

5. Ibid., 43.

6. Aquinas, *Summa Theologica*, Question 58, Article 11.

7. Shamefully, the casuistry of the medieval Catholic Church allowed it to let the Jews become the principal money lenders to merchants and traders, thus piously washing their hands of direct involvement with usurious practices.

Chapter Three / The Evolution of Work

1. Studs Terkel, *Working* (New York: Pantheon Books, 1974), xi.

2. See also chap. 10 for an explanation of the word "economy."

3. The *Oxford Book of Work*, ed. Keith Thomas (New York: Oxford University Press, 1999), xiv.

4. *Laborem Exercens*, text printed in Gregory Baum, *The Priority of Labor* (New York: Paulist Press, 1982), 96.

5. Moses Finley, *Ancient Slavery and Modern Ideology* (New York: Penguin Books, 1983), 67, quoted in Richard Donkin, *Blood, Sweat, and Tears: The Evolution of Work* (New York: Texere, 2001).

6. Lester Little, *Religious Poverty and the Profit Economy in Medieval Europe* (Ithaca, N.Y.: Cornell University Press, 1978), 21.

7. Marc Bloch, *Feudal Society* (New York: Routledge Press, 1989).

8. Charles Dickens, *Hard Times* (London: Penguin Books, 1973), 107.

9. *The Oxford Book of Work*, xiv. I am indebted to its Introduction for the important insights in this paragraph.

10. Dr. Turner Thackrah of Leeds, writing in 1832. Quoted in E. P. Thompson, *The Making of the English Working Class* (New York: Vintage Books, 1966), 329.

11. Ibid., 362.

12. Karl Marx, *Economic and Philosophical Manuscripts*, 1844. Quoted in *The Oxford Book of Work*, 509.

13. Donkin, *Blood, Sweat and Tears*, 138ff.

14. See chap. 2.

15. Henry F. May, *Protestant Churches and Industrial America* (New York: Harper, 1949), 179.

16. "Need for Speed Has Workers Seething," *Los Angeles Times*, June 19, 2002.

17. William Greider, *One World, Ready or Not: The Manic Logic of Global Capitalism* (New York: Touchstone Books, 1997), 20 and 340.

18. Studs Terkel, *Working*, xxxi.

19. Paula Rayman, *Beyond the Bottom Line: The Search for Dignity at Work* (New York: St. Martin's Press, 2001).

Chapter Four / Toward Religious Engagement

1. Quoted in David L. Edwards, ed., *Priests and Workers* (London: SCM Press, 1961).

2. Scott I. Paradise, "A Lesson from a Movement's Demise," *The Witness Magazine*, May 18, 1975.

3. Ibid.

4. Sheffield was the city in the widely acclaimed British film *The Full Monty*, whose central characters were laid-off steelworkers, creatively adapting to new possibilities as the steel industry there collapsed.

5. C. Beales, "Facing the Future," a paper given at an Industrial Mission conference, Hamburg, 1995.

6. Scott I. Paradise, *Detroit Industrial Mission: A Personal Narrative* (New York: Harper & Row, 1968).

Chapter Five / Poverty in History I

1. Quoted in Julio de Santa Ana, *Good News to the Poor* (Maryknoll, N.Y.: Orbis Books, 1979), 68.

2. Brian Tierney, *The Medieval Poor Law* (Berkeley: University of California Press, 1959), chap. 2. I am indebted to Tierney's definitive work on the medieval poor law for much of this section.

3. Ibid., 101 (emphasis added).

4. Barbara Tuchman, *A Distant Mirror: The Calamitous Fourteenth Century* (New York: Ballantine Books, 1978).

5. Tierney, *The Medieval Poor Law*, 109.

6. R. W. Southern, *Western Society and the Church in the Middle Ages* (New York: Penguin Books, 1990), 282.

7. Lester Little, *Religious Poverty and the Profit Economy in Medieval Europe* (Ithaca, N.Y.: Cornell University Press, 1978), 121.

8. Mary T. Malone, *Women of Christianity: From 1000 to the Reformation* (Maryknoll, N.Y.: Orbis Books, 2001). See her chapter on Beguine spirituality.

9. Ibid., 125.

Chapter Six / Poverty in History II

1. From *Selected Sermons of Hugh Latimer*, ed. Allen G. Chester (Charlottesville: University of Virginia Press, 1968), 147–49.

2. Owen Chadwick, *The Reformation* (New York: Penguin Books, 1964; 1990), 184.

3. Vida Scudder, *Socialism and Character* (Boston: Houghton Mifflin, 1912), 132.

4. Chadwick, *The Reformation*, 183.

5. Max Weber, *The Protestant Ethic and the Spirit of Capitalism* (New York: Scribner's, 1976), 113–15.

6. William Temple, *Christianity and Social Order* (1942; New York: Seabury Press reprint, 1977), 51. See his quote at the beginning of chap. 2.

7. R. W. Scribner, "The Reformation Movements in Germany," essay in *The New Cambridge Modern History*, vol. 2, 2nd ed. (Cambridge: Cambridge University Press, 1990), 82.

8. Ibid., 91.

9. Chadwick, *The Reformation*, 193.

10. Christopher Hill, *The World Turned Upside Down* (New York: Viking Press, 1972), 87.

11. Essay by Richard Grassley in *Puritans as Revolutionaries: Essays Presented to Christopher Hill*, ed. Donald Pennington and Keith Thomas (Oxford: Oxford University Press, 1978), 363.

12. Quoted in K. Leech and R. Williams, *Essays Catholic and Radical* (London: Bowerdean Press, 1983), 164–66.

13. Ibid., 167ff.

14. Bernard Kent Markwell, *The Anglican Left: Radical Social Reformers in the Church of England and the Protestant Episcopal Church 1846–1954* (Brooklyn, N.Y.: Carlson, 1991), 166ff.

15. John C. Cort, *Christian Socialism* (Maryknoll, N.Y.: Orbis, 1988), 231–32.

16. Ibid., 327–28.

Chapter Seven / Precursors of Globalization

1. "It's Time to Explore Industrial Policies That Aid Communities," *New York Times*, September 6, 1982.

2. A comprehensive and widely acclaimed book on this subject was Richard J. Barnet and Ronald E. Muller, *Global Reach: The Power of the Multinational Corporations* (New York: Touchstone Books, 1974).

3. Mary Soledad Pepiñan, "One Journey among Others," *International Review of Mission* 73 (1974), 318.

4. Tracy Early, "Corporate Responsibility," *Christianity and Crisis*, March 21, 1978.

Chapter Eight / The New Globalization

1. It is interesting that by 1998, instead of using "West" as a designation for the rich countries, the more common terminology was tending to be "North" for the rich nations and "South" for the poor nations.

2. See chapter 5.

Chapter Nine / The Working Poor in the Global Economy

1. William Greider, *One World, Ready or Not: The Manic Logic of Global Capitalism* (New York: Touchstone Books, 1997), 348.

2. *Boston Globe*, January 12, 2002.

3. Quoted in Henry F. May, *Protestant Churches and Industrial America* (New York: Harper, 1949), 173.

4. "Fair Trade" chocolate can be purchased from Whole Foods stores and other natural food stores. There are Fair Trade cocoa cooperatives, for example, in the Dominican Republic and in Ghana, according to Global Exchange. For details, go to the Global Exchange Web site at *globalexchange.org/cocoa*.

5. "At a Texas Foundry, an Indifference to Life," *New York Times*, January 8, 2003, first of three articles.

6. Congressional Testimony based on "Unfair Advantage: Workers' Freedom of Association in the United States under International Human Rights Standards," August 2000. See Human Rights Watch Web site: *www.hrw.org/reports/2000/uslabor*.

7. Friedman's Golden Straitjacket is the disciplined austerity that poor nations must put on, in the form of deregulation, cuts in social spending, and open markets if they are to prosper in the new globalization. See chapter 1.

8. Quoted in May, *Protestant Churches and Industrial America*, 97.

9. See above page 19.

10. Statement of Appreciation issued by the AFL-CIO, May 1, 2002. See AFL-CIO Web site: *www.aflcio.org* under "Higgins, Msgr. George."

Chapter Ten / Oikonomia *and the Global Household*

1. Lazarus is the poor beggar outside the rich man's gate in Jesus' parable (Luke 16:23).

2. *The Oxford English Dictionary*, 2nd ed. (Oxford: Oxford University Press, 1989).

3. Barbara Garson, *Money Makes the World Go Around* (New York: Viking/Penguin, 2001).

4. Kevin Phillips, *Arrogant Capital* (Boston: Little, Brown, 1994), 82.

5. See chap. 7.

6. Amartya Sen, "How to Judge Globalism," special issue on globalism, *The American Prospect* (Winter 2002), A4.

7. Richard Parker, "Globalization," address to the Episcopal House of Bishops, September 27, 2001.

8. Matthew Bishop, "Capitalism and Its Troubles," *The Economist*, May 18, 2002, 6.

9. Laurie Green, *The Impact of the Global: An Urban Theology* (London: Anglican Urban Network, 2001), 11, 12.

10. Saskia Sassen, "Toward a Feminist Analytics of the Global Economy," in *Globalization and Its Discontents* (New York: The New Press, 1998), 86.

11. Kenneth Leech, *Through Our Long Exile* (London: Darton, Longman, and Todd, 2001), 222.

12. Julio de Santa Ana, *Good News to the Poor* (Maryknoll, N.Y.: Orbis Books, 1979), 40.

13. R. H. Tawney, *Religion and the Rise of Capitalism* (1926; New Brunswick, N.J.: Transaction, 1998), 31 (emphasis added).

14. Lester Little, *Religious Poverty and the Profit Economy in Medieval Europe* (Ithaca, N.Y.: Cornell University Press, 1978), 36.

15. F. D. Maurice, *The Kingdom of Christ*, vol. 2 (London: SCM Press, 1958), 86.

16. See chap. 6.

17. Green, *The Impact of the Global*, 32.

Chapter Eleven / Public Policy Choices in the New Global Economic Order

1. Joseph E. Stiglitz, *Globalization and Its Discontents* (New York: W. W. Norton, 2002), 9.

2. Bill Moyers on *NOW*, PBS documentary, September 5, 2003.

3. "The Rigged Trade Game," *New York Times*, editorial, July 20, 2003.

4. "Latino Immigrants Pay a Price for Free Trade," *Los Angeles Times*, June 12, 2001.

5. See chapter 8.

6. William Greider, *One World, Ready or Not: The Manic Logic of Global Capitalism* (New York: Touchstone Books, 1997), 317.

7. Ersline Childers and Brian Urquhart, "Renewing the United Nations System, 1994," cited in *Alternatives to Economic Globalization: A Better World Is Possible*, a Report of the International Forum on Globalization (San Francisco: Berrett-Koehler Publications, 2002), 221.

8. Interview with Anuradha Mittal, in *Multinational Monitor*, July–August, 2003, 30–33.

9. See chapter 8.

10. David C. Korten, *The Post-Corporate World: Life after Capitalism* (West Hartford, Conn.: Kumarian Press, and San Francisco: Berrett-Koehler Publishers, 1999), 184.

11. Charles Kingsley, *Charles Kingsley: His Letters and Memories of His Life*, 4th ed., ed. Frances Eliza Grenfell Kingsley (New York: Scribner's, 1877), 76–77.

12. *Alternatives to Economic Globalization*, 61.

Chapter Twelve / Making Connections with the Global

1. *Global Civil Society 2003*, the third annual report of the Center for Civil Society and the Center for the Study of Global Governance, London School of Economics, Oxford University Press, 2003.

2. Ibid., 4.

3. In Saskia Sassen, *Globalization and Its Discontents* (New York: The New Press, 1998), 86.

4. This dramatic story is told by David Bacon in *Labor Notes* (July 2002).

5. See chap. 7.

6. See *www.naugatuckvalleyproject.org* for goals and projects.

7. Another principal globalization theme, global debt, was discussed in chap. 8.

8. See *www.ecupres.com.ar/download/documentos/PreDoc%20143.doc* (document in Spanish; quotation above translated by the author).

9. Pamela Brubaker, "Report from the WCC/WB/IMF Encounter," *Journal of Lutheran Ethics* (December 2003).

Chapter Thirteen / Another World Is Possible

1. As the nineteenth-century Anglican theologian F. D. Maurice expressed it. See chap. 10.

2. James O. S. Huntington, *Bargainers and Beggars: A Study of the Parable of the Laborers in the Vineyard* (West Park, N.Y.: Holy Cross Press, 1919), 11.

3. The Medellín (Colombia) conference of Latin American Bishops in 1968 gave prominence to this phrase, a prominence unfortunately subsequently downplayed by the Catholic Church.

4. Paul F. Knitter and Chandra Muzaffar, eds., *Subverting Greed: Religious Perspectives on the Global Economy* (Maryknoll, N.Y.: Orbis Books, 2002). This is an eminently useful book in bringing together the major religious traditions and their perspectives on globalization.

5. See the excellent Jewish bimonthly magazine *Tikkun.*

6. In Knitter and Muzaffar, *Subverting Greed*, chap. 7, 143.

7. In J. Sobrino and F. Wilfred, eds., *Globalization and Its Victims*, Concilium 2001/5 (London: SCM Press, 2001).

8. Knitter and Muzaffar, *Subverting Greed,* 162, 163.

9. Harvey Cox, "The Market as God," *Atlantic Monthly* (March 1999), 18.

10. Philip Bobbitt, a leading constitutional theorist, teaches law at the University of Texas. He is the author of *The Shield of Achilles: War, Peace, and the Course of History* (New York: Knopf, 2002).

11. The introduction and the entire document can be found at the Web site *www.whitehouse.gov/nsc/nss.html.*

12. Ibid., pages 17 and 18 of this section (PDF format).

13. In Amartya Sen, "How to Judge Globalism," *The American Prospect* (Winter 2002), A3. Sen, the 1998 Nobel Laureate in economic science, is a native of India. See also chap. 10.

14. Canon John Atherton, Manchester Cathedral, "Changing Church and Society: From William Temple to the 21st Century," unpublished paper, March 2001.

15. Here are four organizations helpful for community organizing, and their Web sites: (1) The Citizen's Handbook: A Guide to Building Community (*vcn.bc.ca/ citizens-handbook*); (2) Comm-Org: Online Conference on Community Organizing and Development (*comm-org.utoledo.edu*); (3) The Interreligious Foundation for Community Organizing (*ifconews.org*); (4) the Maryknoll Sisters (Roman Catholic) Web site (*maryknoll.org/index*), especially good on global issues.

16. Bitter herbs and milk and honey are part of the Jewish Passover meal to recall to the faithful the memory of the slavery of the Israelites in Egypt, and their deliverance to the Promised Land. Three weeks after this Beverly Hills march the recalcitrant hotel signed the new labor contract.

Bibliography

Note: Some listings in each of the three sections below overlap in subject matter, e.g., some listings in church history/theology may have globalization and/or labor themes.

Church History and Theology

Beales, C. "Facing the Future," a paper given at an Industrial Mission conference, Hamburg, 1995.

Bigongiari, Dino, ed. *The Political Ideas of St. Thomas Aquinas.* New York: Hafner Press, 9th printing, 1973.

Bloch, Marc. *Feudal Society.* New York: Routledge Press, 1989.

Bossy, John. *Christianity in the West, 1400–1700.* New York: Oxford University Press, 1985.

Brubaker, Pamela K. *Globalization at What Price?* Cleveland: Pilgrim Press, 2001.

———. "Report from the WCC/WB/IMF Encounter." *Journal of Lutheran Ethics* (December 2003).

Cambridge Economic History of Europe. *Economic Organization and Policies in the Middle Ages.* Vol. 3. Cambridge: Cambridge University Press, 1963. See chapter 8, "Conceptions of Economy and Society," 555–75.

Chadwick, Owen. *The Reformation.* New York: Penguin Books, 1964; 1990.

Chester, Allen G., ed. *Selected Sermons of Hugh Latimer.* Charlottesville: University of Virginia Press, 1968.

Cort, John C. *Christian Socialism.* Maryknoll, N.Y.: Orbis Books, 1988.

De Santa Ana, Julio. *Good News to the Poor.* Maryknoll, N.Y.: Orbis Books, 1979.

Dorrien, Gary. *Reconstructing the Common Good.* Maryknoll, N.Y.: Orbis Books, 1990.

Edwards, David L., ed. *Priests and Workers.* London: SCM Press, 1961.

Ely, Richard T. *Ground under Our Feet.* New York: Macmillan, 1938.

Forell, George W., ed. *Christian Social Teachings: A Reader.* Minneapolis: Augsburg, 1966.

Gore, Charles. "Christ and Society." Lectures at St. Botolph's Church, Bishopsgate, London, 1927.

———, ed. *Property and Its Duties and Rights, Historically, Philosophically and Religiously Regarded.* New York: Macmillan, 1915.

Green, Laurie. *The Impact of the Global: An Urban Theology.* London: Anglican Urban Network, London, 2001.

Hill, Christopher. *The World Turned Upside Down*. New York: Viking Press, 1972.

Jarl, Ann-Cathrin. *In Justice: Women and Global Economics*. Minneapolis: Fortress Press, 2003.

Kinsler, Gloria, and Ross Kinsler. *The Biblical Jubilee and the Struggle for Life*. Maryknoll, N.Y.: Orbis Books, 1999.

Knitter, Paul F., and Chandra Muzaffar, eds. *Subverting Greed: Religious Perspectives on the Global Economy*. Maryknoll, N.Y.: Orbis Books, 2002.

Leech, Kenneth. *Through Our Long Exile*. London: Darton, Longman, and Todd, 2001.

Leech, Kenneth, and Rowan Williams. *Essays Catholic and Radical*. London: Bowerdean Press, 1983.

Lindberg, Carter. *Beyond Charity: Reformation Initiatives for the Poor*. Minneapolis: Fortress Press, 1993.

Little, Lester. *Religious Poverty and the Profit Economy in Medieval Europe*. Ithaca, N.Y.: Cornell University Press, 1978.

Malone, Mary T. *Women of Christianity: From 1000 to the Reformation*. Maryknoll, N.Y.: Orbis Books, 2001.

Markwell, Bernard Kent. *The Anglican Left: Radical Social Reformers in the Church of England and the Protestant Episcopal Church 1846–1954*. Brooklyn, N.Y.: Carlson, 1991.

Maurice, F. D. *The Kingdom of Christ*. London: SCM Press, 1958.

May, Henry F. *Protestant Churches and Industrial America*. New York: Harper, 1949.

McFague, Sallie. *Life Abundant: Rethinking Theology and Economy for a Planet in Peril*. Minneapolis: Fortress Press, 2001.

Moe-Lobeda, Cynthia. *Healing a Broken World: Globalization and God*. Minneapolis: Fortress Press, 2002.

Myers, Ched. *The Biblical Vision of Sabbath Economics*. Washington, D.C.: Tell the World, Church of the Saviour, 2001.

Oliver, John. *The Church and Social Order: Social Thought in the Church of England 1918–1939*. London: Mowbrays, 1968.

Paradise, Scott I. *Detroit Industrial Mission: A Personal Narrative*. New York: Harper and Row, 1968.

———."A Lesson from a Movement's Demise." *The Witness Magazine*, May 18, 1975.

Rauschenbusch, Walter. *Christianity and the Social Crisis*. New York: Macmillan, 1907.

———. *Christianizing the Social Order*. New York: Macmillan, 1912.

Roosevelt, Theodore. *The Foes of Our Own Household*. New York: George H. Doran, 1917.

Scribner, R. W. "The Reformation Movements in Germany," essay in *The New Cambridge Modern History*. Vol. 2. 2nd ed. Cambridge: Cambridge University Press, 1990.

Scudder, Vida. *Socialism and Character.* Boston: Houghton Mifflin, 1912.

Sobrino, Jon, and Felix Wilfred, eds. *Globalization and Its Victims.* Concilium 2001/5. London: SCM Press, 2001.

Southern, R. W. *Western Society and the Church in the Middle Ages.* New York: Penguin Books, 1990.

Tanner, Kathryn. *Jesus, Humanity, and the Trinity.* Minneapolis: Fortress Press, 2003.

Tawney, R. H. *Religion and the Rise of Capitalism.* New Brunswick, N.J.: Transaction, 1998.

Temple, William. *Christianity and Social Order.* 1942. Reprint, New York: Seabury Press, 1977.

Tierney, Brian. *The Medieval Poor Law.* Berkeley: University of California Press, 1959.

Troeltsch, Ernst. *The Social Teaching of the Christian Churches.* 2 vols. London and New York: Macmillan, 1931.

Tuchman, Barbara. *A Distant Mirror: The Calamitous Fourteenth Century.* New York: Ballantine Books, 1978.

Weber, Max. *The Protestant Ethic and the Spirit of Capitalism.* New York: Scribner's, 1976.

Wickham, E. R. *Church and People in an Industrial City.* London: Lutterworth Press, 1957.

Wollenberg, Bruce. *Christian Social Thought in Great Britain between the Wars.* Lanham, Md.: University Press of America, 1997.

Economics and Globalization

Alternatives to Economic Globalization: A Report of the International Forum on Globalization. San Francisco: Berrett-Koehler Publishers, 2000.

Barber, Benjamin. *Jihad vs. McWorld: How Globalism and Tribalism Are Reshaping the World.* New York: Ballantine Books, 1996.

Barlow, Maude, and Tony Clarke. *Blue Gold: The Battle against Corporate Theft of the World's Water.* New York: New Press, 2002.

Barnet, Richard J., and Ronald E. Muller. *Global Reach: The Power of the Multinational Corporations.* New York: Touchstone Books, 1974.

Bishop, Matthew. "Capitalism and Its Troubles." *The Economist,* May 18, 2002.

Bobbitt, Philip. *The Shield of Achilles: War, Peace, and the Course of History.* New York: Knopf, 2002.

Braudel, Fernand. *Civilization and Capitalism: 15th–18th Century.* 3 vols., English trans. New York: Harper and Row, 1981.

Childers, Ersline, and Brian Urquhart. "Renewing the United Nations System, 1994." In *Alternatives to Economic Globalization: A Better World Is Possible,* a Report of the International Forum on Globalization. San Francisco: Berrett-Koehler Publications, 2002.

Cox, Harvey. "The Market as God." *Atlantic Monthly* (March 1999).

Daly, Herman E., and John B. Cobb Jr. *For the Common Good: Redirecting the Economy toward Community, the Environment, and a Sustainable Future.* Boston: Beacon Press, 1994.

Duchrow, Ulrich, and Franz J. Hinkelammert. *Property for People, Not for Profit: Alternatives to the Global Tyranny of Capital.* London: Zed Books, 2004.

Early, Tracy. "Corporate Responsibility." *Christianity and Crisis*, March 21, 1978.

Friedman, Thomas L. *The Lexus and the Olive Tree.* Rev. ed. New York: Anchor Books, 2000.

Fukuyama, Francis. *The End of History and the Last Man.* New York: Free Press, 1992.

Garson, Barbara. *Money Makes the World Go Around.* New York: Viking/Penguin Books, 2001.

Global Civil Society 2003, a report of the Center for Civil Society and the Center for the Study of Global Governance, London School of Economics. New York: Oxford University Press, 2003.

Global Economic Prospects and Developing Countries. Washington, D.C.: World Bank, 2000.

Greider, William. *One World, Ready or Not: The Manic Logic of Global Capitalism.* New York: Touchstone Books, 1997.

———. *The Soul of Capitalism.* New York: Simon and Schuster, 2003.

Heilbroner, Robert F. *The Essential Adam Smith.* New York: Norton, 1986.

Jardine, Murray. *The Making and Unmaking of Technological Society: How Christianity Can Save Modernity from Itself.* Grand Rapids: Brazos Press, 2004.

Klein, Naomi. *No Logo: Taking Aim at the Brand Bullies.* New York: Picador USA, 2000.

Korten, David C. *The Post-Corporate World: Life after Capitalism.* West Hartford, Conn.: Kumarian Press, and San Francisco: Berrett-Koehler Publications, 1999.

"Latino Immigrants Pay a Price for Free Trade." *Los Angeles Times*, June 12, 2001.

Mander, Jerry, and Edward Goldsmith, eds. *The Case Against the Global Economy.* San Francisco: Sierra Club Books, 1996.

Mumford, Lewis. *The Pentagon of Power: The Myth of the Machine.* New York: Harcourt Brace Jovanovich, 1970.

Parker, Richard. "Globalization," address to the Episcopal House of Bishops, September 27, 2001.

Pepiñan, Mary Soledad. "One Journey among Others." *International Review of Mission* 73 (1974).

Phillips, Kevin. *Arrogant Capital.* Boston: Little, Brown, 1994.

———. *Wealth and Democracy: A Political History of the American Rich.* New York: Broadway Books, 2002.

Pollin, Robert, and Stephanie Luce. *The Living Wage: Building a Fair Economy.* New York: New Press, 1998.

"The Rigged Trade Game." *New York Times*, editorial, July 20, 2003.

Robinson, William G. "Globalisation: Nine Theses on Our Epoch." *Race and Class* 38, no. 2 (1996).

Sassen, Saskia. *Cities in a World Economy.* 2nd ed. Thousand Oaks, Calif.: Pine Forge Press, 2002.

——. *Globalization and Its Discontents* (New York: The New Press, 1998).

Sen, Amartya. "How to Judge Globalism." *The American Prospect* (Winter 2002).

Shipler, David K. *The Working Poor: Invisible in America.* New York: Alfred A. Knopf, 2004.

Shiva, Vandana. *Stolen Harvest: The Hijacking of the Global Food Supply.* Cambridge, Mass.: South End Press, 1999.

Soros, George. *The Crisis of Global Capitalism.* New York: Public Affairs Books, 1998.

——. *George Soros on Globalization.* New York: Public Affairs Books, 2002.

Stiglitz, Joseph E. *Globalization and Its Discontents.* New York: W. W. Norton, 2002.

Weisbrot, Mark. "The Mirage of Progress: The Economic Failure of the Last Two Decades of the Twentieth Century." *The American Prospect* (Winter 2002).

Yergin, Daniel, and Joseph Stanislaw. *The Commanding Heights: The Battle for the World Economy.* New York: Touchstone Books, 1998.

Work and Labor

Adler, William M. *Mollie's Job: A Story of Life and Work on the Global Assembly Line.* New York: Touchstone Books, 2001.

Aronowitz, Stanley. *Working Class Hero.* Cleveland: Pilgrim Press, 1983.

Donkin, Richard. *Blood, Sweat, and Tears: The Evolution of Work.* New York: Texere, 2001.

Dulles, Foster Rhea. *Labor in America, a History.* 3rd ed. New York: Thomas Y. Crowell, 1966.

Ehrenreich, Barbara. *Nickel and Dimed: On (Not) Getting by in America.* New York: Metropolitan Books, 2001.

Finley, Moses. *Ancient Slavery and Modern Ideology.* New York: Penguin Books, 1983.

Gig: Americans Talk about Their Jobs at the Turn of the Millennium. Ed. John Bowe et al. New York: Crown Publishers, 2000.

Gillett, Richard W. *The Human Enterprise: A Christian Perspective on Work.* Kansas City, Mo.: Leaven Press, 1985.

Huntington, James O. S. *Bargainers and Beggars: A Study of the Parable of the Laborers in the Vineyard.* West Park, N.Y.: Holy Cross Press, 1919.

Hondagnew-Sotelo, Pierrette. *Doméstica: Immigrant Workers Cleaning and Caring in the Shadows of Affluence.* Berkeley: University of California Press, 2001.

Kingsley, Charles. *Charles Kingsley: His Letters and Memories of His Life.* 4th ed. Ed. Frances Eliza Grenfell Kingsley. New York: Scribner's, 1877.

Laborem Exercens, Papal Encyclical of John Paul II. Text printed in Gregory Baum, *The Priority of Labor.* New York: Paulist Press, 1982.

Moyers, Bill. *NOW,* PBS documentary, September 5, 2003.

Murolo, Priscilla, and A. B. Chitty. *From the Folks Who Brought You the Weekend: A Short, Illustrated History of Labor in the United States.* New York: New Press, 2001.

Rayman, Paula. *Beyond the Bottom Line: The Search for Dignity at Work.* New York: St. Martin's Press, 2001.

Rifkin, Jeremy. *The End of Work.* New York: G. P. Putman & Sons, 1996.

Teaching for Change: Popular Education and the Labor Movement. Ed. Kent Wong et al. Los Angeles: UCLA Center for Labor Research and Education, 2002.

Terkel, Studs. *Working.* New York: Pantheon Books, 1974.

Theriault, Reg. *How to Tell When You're Tired: A Brief Examination of Work.* New York: W. W. Norton, 1995.

Thomas, Keith, ed. *The Oxford Book of Work.* New York: Oxford University Press, 1999.

Thompson, E. P. *The Making of the English Working Class.* New York: Vintage Books, 1966.

United for a Fair Economy. *The Growing Divide: Inequality and the Roots of Economic Insecurity.* Boston: United for a Fair Economy, November 2001.

Index